Jan–Apr 2024

Day by Day with God

Rooting women's lives in the Bible

BRF
Ministries

 Ministries

15 The Chambers, Vineyard
Abingdon OX14 3FE
brf.org.uk

Bible Reading Fellowship is a charity (233280)
and company limited by guarantee (301324),
registered in England and Wales

ISBN 978 1 80039 256 4
All rights reserved

Distributed in Australia by:
MediaCom Education Inc, PO Box 610, Unley, SA 5061
Tel: 1 800 811 311 | admin@mediacom.org.au

Distributed in New Zealand by:
Scripture Union Wholesale, PO Box 760, Wellington
Tel: 04 385 0421 | suwholesale@clear.net.nz

Acknowledgements
Scripture quotations marked with the following abbreviations are taken from the version shown. Where no abbreviation is given, the quotation is taken from the same version as the headline reference. NLT: The Holy Bible, New Living Translation, copyright © 1996, 2004, 2007, 2013. Used by permission of Tyndale House Publishers, Inc., Carol Stream, Illinois 60188. All rights reserved. NRSV: The New Revised Standard Version of the Bible, Anglicised edition, copyright © 1989, 1995 by the Division of Christian Education of the National Council of the Churches of Christ in the United States of America. Used by permission. All rights reserved. NIV: The Holy Bible, New International Version (Anglicised edition) copyright © 1979, 1984, 2011 by Biblica. Used by permission of Hodder & Stoughton Publishers, a Hachette UK company. All rights reserved. 'NIV' is a registered trademark of Biblica. UK trademark number 1448790. MSG: *The Message*, copyright © 1993, 1994, 1995, 1996, 2000, 2001, 2002 by Eugene H. Peterson. Used by permission of NavPress. All rights reserved. Represented by Tyndale House Publishers, Inc. TLB: The Living Bible copyright © 1971 by Tyndale House Foundation. Used by permission of Tyndale House Publishers Inc., Carol Stream, Illinois 60188. All rights reserved. NKJV: The New King James Version®. Copyright © 1982 by Thomas Nelson. Used by permission. All rights reserved.

A catalogue record for this book is available from the British Library

Printed and bound by Gutenberg Press, Tarxien, Malta

Day by Day
with
God

Edited by **Jackie Harris**   January–April 2024

6   Joseph: a life of ups and downs
Di Archer   *1–13 January*

20   God of the wind and rain
Sara Batts-Neale   *14–20 January*

28   The letters of John
Rosemary Green   *21 January–3 February*

43   How to pray for our leaders
Catherine Larner   *4–10 February*

51   Singleness, through the lens of the Bible
Ruth Akinradewo   *11–24 February*

66   Psalm 37: how to live in an imperfect world
Jackie Harris   *25 February–2 March*

74   The names of God
Chine McDonald   *3–16 March*

89   Hosea: God's redeeming love (part 1)
Helen Williams   *17–23 March*

97   Jesus, the Messiah
Jane Walters   *24 March–6 April*

112   What does it mean to be a 'living sacrifice'?
Lyndall Bywater   *7–20 April*

127   Our favourite characters
Ensemble   *21–30 April*

Writers in this issue

Di Archer is CEO of **tastelifeuk.org**, a charity she cofounded after family experience of eating disorders. An educator, writer and speaker, she is also resources manager on the CPAS leadership training team.

Revd Dr Sara Batts-Neale is a priest in the diocese of Chelmsford. She is currently the Anglican chaplain to the University of Essex. Married to Tim, they live with a dog and host a cat.

Rosemary Green lives in Abingdon, where her ministry as a layperson is mainly among the elderly. A grandmother and great-grandmother, she loves trying to make the Bible alive and relevant to BRF readers.

Catherine Larner is a freelance writer, editor and presenter who reports on literature, culture and faith for national, regional and Christian magazines and local radio.

Ruth Akinradewo is a self-described laugh-aholic and Jesus addict, who advocates for the voiceless – particularly for victims of domestic abuse, as a trustee for Beauty for Ashes Refuges. Ruth leads worship regularly at her church.

Chine McDonald is director of the religion and society think tank Theos. A regular contributor to BBC religion and ethics programmes, she also sits on several charity boards. She is married to Mark, and they have two little boys.

Helen Williams has worked in music, education, management consultancy and administration. She currently finds herself working mostly alongside her husband, an Anglican bishop, while continuing to work as an accompanist.

Jane Walters is an author, speaker and musician based in Norfolk. She is chair of the Association of Christian Writers and leads two local affiliated writing groups, as well as facilitating Christian writing retreats further afield. **janewyattwalters.com**

Lyndall Bywater lives in Canterbury and works with The Salvation Army and the diocese of Canterbury, helping people pray. She is the author of two books, both published by BRF: *Faith in the Making* and *Prayer in the Making*.

Welcome

Happy New Year! We're excited to share God's word with you as we move into 2024. Whether you have been reading your Bible for years or are just beginning to establish a daily routine, we hope these notes will nourish and inspire you.

I must confess I haven't always been disciplined in my Bible study, but joining the team at BRF has really helped me to rediscover the joy of spending time in God's word. It's amazing how sometimes studies I commissioned or edited months ago minister to me as I use them as part of my own quiet time or even as I am working on them.

In the weeks I was editing this issue, my sister was rushed to hospital with pneumonia and sepsis and put in an induced coma. The day I heard the news I was working on Chine's study on the names of God and found it both a comfort and an inspiration as to how to pray for the situation. Thankfully, God brought my sister through that ordeal, and throughout those weeks there were nuggets either in the studies I was editing or in the daily notes that gave me hope or something to focus on.

As I have read through this issue again, I realise there is a lot about dealing with difficult or challenging situations. We begin with the story of Joseph and how God was with him throughout all the twists and turns in his life. We consider what the Bible teaches us about praying for our leaders and living as single people, and we delve into a psalm that teaches us how to live in an imperfect world. Elsewhere, we focus on God's love as revealed through the prophet Hosea, listen to what Matthew tells us about Jesus, the Messiah, and ponder what it means to be a 'living sacrifice'. Whatever you are facing in the next few weeks and months, I pray that you will find something in these notes that will speak to you.

There is just space to introduce a new contributor to our team of writers. Jane Walters is a Christian writer and speaker, based in Norfolk. She says she loves making the Bible accessible and helping readers to connect with both its stories and the God who appears behind and through them all.

As we spend time together in God's word, may we be able to make that connection and let his word shape what we think and are, and what we do.

Jackie Harris, Editor

Joseph: a life of ups and downs

Di Archer writes:

The story of Joseph and his coat of many colours may be one of the few biblical stories still vaguely in the consciousness of the general public – many may well remember the relaunched stage show *Joseph and the Amazing Technicolour Dreamcoat*. Some, like my husband, may even know the lyrics and music to it off by heart. It is a story of high drama, clear 'goodies' and 'baddies', unexpected twists and deep family trauma which is more than worthy of being brought to the stage. Reading the original story in a translation of the Bible which is comfortable for you is no less dramatic. Indeed, it is written in a way that catches our attention, as it unrolls before us like a gripping soap opera.

There are so many universal themes that we can relate to in this powerful story. We may not have been physically dumped, coat-less, into a water well, but most of us have known times of betrayal in other ways – or of being trapped with no guarantee of a future. Few of us survive family life without some darker emotions and difficulties threatening our emotional health. Some of us do get involved in world events and may have influence we can use, as Joseph did. Are we doing so with comparable wisdom? All of us are affected by circumstances around us, just as Joseph was.

Starting a new year with Joseph will hopefully be an encouragement to us. Much as we sincerely pray that the coming days will be calm and happy, we know all too well that there will be both challenges and joys ahead. This is how life is. Accepting the ups and downs, and walking through all of them with Jesus, is easier said than done. Joseph's ultimate reminder to us is that, while circumstances can look really bad, God is always working for our good within them. This is a rock-solid reassurance to take into the coming year. Many of us, however, find it hard to hold on to. My prayer is that, over the next few days of tracing Joseph's story, we will learn from him some new ways of recognising how close God is to us, at all times, and what it means for us that he always has our good in mind.

Love and clothes

Jacob loved Joseph more than any of his other children because Joseph had been born to him in his old age. So one day Jacob had a special gift made for Joseph – a beautiful robe. But his brothers hated Joseph because their father loved him more than the rest of them. They couldn't say a kind word to him. (vv. 3–4, NLT)

We are flung straight into the drama as the 17-year-old shepherd Joseph tells on his half-brothers: 'But Joseph reported to his father some of the bad things his brothers were doing' (v. 2). I wonder what those bad things were. Were they selling fleeces on the side, to line their own pockets? Were they ill-treating the sheep? From his behaviour later in the story, I imagine that Joseph was worried, rather than simply trying to get his brothers into trouble. But he was on the back foot from the start – everyone knew he was the favourite son of his father Jacob's favourite wife, Rachel, now deceased. Not only that, but he had also been given a stunningly beautiful coat, which was symbolic of Jacob's decision to bequeath a major part of his inheritance to him.

Sibling relationships can be complex enough in a straightforward family, let alone in a blended one like Joseph's. We are so prone to jealously and insecurity. Are we loved as much as our sisters and brothers? What is our place? Why do we so often feel misunderstood? Why are our achievements sometimes not prized as much as others? It is so easy for these unhelpful thoughts and feelings to creep in.

Joseph, in his immaturity and enthusiasm, presumably had no idea that sharing his dreams of stars, moon and sheaves would inflame an already volatile situation. Perhaps he was excited that he and his brothers would share a great future – after all, they were all to be stars and fruitful farmers! He was too young to realise that his brothers would only see the negative implications of Joseph's centre-stage role.

Dear Father, thank you that your plans for me are for my good. Help me to trust your word in this for the year ahead. Amen..

DI ARCHER

The well of pain

Then the brothers killed a young goat and dipped Joseph's robe in its blood. They sent the beautiful robe to their father… Their father recognised it immediately. 'Yes,' he said, 'it is my son's robe. A wild animal must have eaten him. Joseph has clearly been torn to pieces!' (vv. 31–33, NLT)

The problems in Joseph's family spilled over into horrific violence against him. It may be hard for us to appreciate just how bad the relationships had deteriorated, but it can happen. When people feel threatened, unloved, unsupported or unfairly treated, the repercussions can be very difficult. They may not be murderous, but they can be.

Joseph was within moments of losing his life – perhaps it was the build-up of frustration with him; perhaps it was the hope that the inheritance would be more fairly shared without him; perhaps his half-brothers egged each other on. Joseph's pleading for his life fell on deaf ears (see Genesis 42:21). Whatever the reason, without the interference of Reuben and Judah, that would have been the end of Joseph's story. As it was, even Reuben's plan to rescue Joseph from the well was thwarted. The soaking of the beautiful coat in goat's blood was in response to Reuben's despair.

Betrayal from those nearest and dearest to us is the worst kind of betrayal. Many of us may have experienced this in one way or another. Some of us may have been the cause of it. Jacob's family feuds were messy, deep-seated and very real. Ours can be as well. Family feuds include those in the church family too. I have heard it said that there is no pain like church pain. When those we value the most and trust the most betray us, it can feel unbearable.

Being sold to the foreign traders instead of being killed was definitely a good thing for Joseph, but still unbelievably traumatic for a young man wrenched from the security of being the beloved son. Yet we know that God was with him, even in these awful developments, as God is with you.

Pray for unity and grace in your church family. If you are facing the fallout from relationship betrayal right now, please talk to someone. Let a friend walk beside you to carry and process the pain.

DI ARCHER

Potiphar's house and wife

But Joseph refused. 'Look,' he told her, 'my master trusts me with everything in his entire household. No one here has more authority than I do. He has held back nothing from me except you, because you are his wife. How could I do such a wicked thing? It would be a great sin against God.' (vv. 8–9, NLT)

Chained up and sold in an Egyptian slave market, Joseph must have been terrified. Purchased by the influential Potiphar, Pharaoh's captain of the guard, Joseph was now owned, body and soul, by another human being. He had no rights, family, standing or voice.

So, he had to choose. Would he sink into despair and depression, allowing his circumstances to overwhelm him? Would he perform his obligatory duties sullenly and resentfully? It doesn't seem so. Admirably, he went about his tasks without rancour and was put in charge of the household, thus incurring God's blessing. We are reassured that 'the Lord was with Joseph, giving him success' (v. 3). Did Joseph sense that presence with him? He could certainly tell his life was improving.

Then it fell apart. He admirably refused Potiphar's wife's advances and again was unfairly betrayed and flung into bondage. He lost another coat. But Joseph had learned his lesson. If God could be with him as a slave, God could be with him as a prisoner. The 'success' that God gave him may not have been highly rated in worldly terms, but it was enough for Joseph.

The challenge for us is obvious. When life throws us curve balls, as Joseph's did for him, how do we respond? Do we allow God to give us his type of 'success'? Do we choose to do right, resist resentment and bitterness, and look for God's presence, even in the most unwelcome circumstances? I do not want to be glib about this. Perhaps Joseph had to wrestle his way into trust and obedience. Talking to a friend recently whose husband had abandoned her, I was in awe of her painful journey through anguish and tears to a place where she deliberately chooses, day by day, to live without anger, recognising that this way, she is free.

Dear Father, it is not easy to keep trusting you when life is difficult. Thank you that you are no stranger to pain. Please help us to find you even when we are hurting and afraid. Amen..

DI ARCHER

No guarantees

'And please remember me and do me a favour when things go well for you. Mention me to Pharaoh, so he might let me out of this place. For I was kidnapped from my homeland, the land of the Hebrews, and now I'm here in prison, but I did nothing to deserve it.' (vv. 14–15, NLT)

Surely Joseph must have thought his day had come, when he correctly interpreted his fellow prisoners' dreams, and knew that the soon-to-be-reinstated chief cupbearer would have the ear of the king. He had even passed the test of how to deliver his interpretations; he must have taken a deep breath before sharing his understanding of the ill-fated baker's dream. But he did it anyway, perhaps with more sensitivity than he ever showed his brothers in the past. He must then have held his breath every day for a while before he realised that the cupbearer had forgotten all about him. Joseph's prison trial continued for another two years.

It is incredibly hard to keep going when you are waiting for circumstances to improve, or longed-for events to come to pass. It is very difficult to contain worry for people you love and fears for the future. The fact that Joseph kept on doing the right thing every day – caring for others, being responsible, putting one dogged foot in front of the other – is meant to inspire us to do the same. In recognising the challenge of this, do you know what helps you to keep on keeping on? If you are facing tough stuff, can you explore some new ways to help you thrive, or at least survive, spiritually, emotionally and physically, even in the midst of it all? Conversely, if you are cruising through life at the moment, what can you put in place to make the most of that, for yourself and others? Do you have helpful habits to sustain you into and beyond a future hard time? It's so much better to have our resources amassed before the crises arrive. And just like Joseph, God is always with us.

Read Luke 12:32. God is always on your side, and he is happy to be there.

DI ARCHER

Joseph's superpower

**'God has revealed to Pharaoh in advance what he is about to do. The
next seven years will be a period of great prosperity throughout the
land of Egypt. But afterward there will be seven years of famine so
great that all the prosperity will be forgotten in Egypt.'** (vv. 28–30, NLT)

Two years was a long time for Joseph to contemplate the accuracy of his
dream interpretation on God's behalf. He had been careful to underline to
the baker and the cupbearer that his skill at interpreting was not his, but
God's (40:8), but others must surely have seen it as a bit of a superpower.
Thus, when Pharoah started having disturbing dreams, the cupbearer
remembered Joseph.

This was the moment when Joseph's life changed yet again, and
more obviously for the better. He was made presentable (a decent coat
perhaps?) and hauled before Pharoah. Despite the imposing surround-
ings, which must have been such a contrast to his prison, Joseph stood
his ground, insisting that it was the power of God that Pharoah needed
to interpret the dreams. Having had practice in bearing bad news, he did
not flinch from telling Pharoah what he did not want to hear –that famine
was on the way. He also advised him that he should prepare for this by
appointing a suitable wise manager to manage the storage of crops for the
future seven years of famine.

Did Joseph make this suggestion hoping that he would be just that
man? Was he that shrewd? It was a good idea either way, and he would
not have been assigned the role had he not already proven himself as trust-
worthy, diligent and wise. Those long years of containment and hardship
had prepared him for this moment, and he was ready. Verse 46 tells us that
Joseph was 30 years old when he started working for Pharoah. He had 13
years of training in slavery and prison, alone in a foreign land, before this
happened. Symbolising his rise to a position of authority, Joseph was given
new clothing, made of fine linen. This time he got to keep it.

---

*Joseph would go on to avert a national crisis and secure Egypt's future.
How open are you to God working through you to bless others, whatever
that may mean?*

DI ARCHER

11

Moving on

Two sons were born to Joseph and his wife, Asenath… Joseph named his older son Manasseh, for he said, 'God has made me forget all my troubles and everyone in my father's family.' Joseph named his second son Ephraim, for he said, 'God has made me fruitful in this land of my grief.' (vv. 50–52, NLT)

Life changed dramatically for Joseph as he began the monumental task of saving a nation from future starvation. He was given full authority by Pharoah to do what was necessary and started the plan with his customary care and conscientiousness. During this time, he also married and had two sons. He was aware of these as compensating blessings for his very real years of suffering, saying, 'God has made me fruitful in this land of my grief' (v. 52). I can't help thinking that he was a little unrealistic in naming his first son Manasseh. He clearly did not forget everyone in his father's family, as he was soon to find out.

It might have been better had he acknowledged the trauma he had been through in being snatched from his childhood so roughly. But the Egyptian ruling class were probably not into emotional development. Certainly, Joseph was attempting to move on and make the most of his new and extraordinary circumstances, with much of his day-to-day struggle now alleviated. It would have been churlish of him not to do so. He held firm to his trust in God in the names he gave his boys and did not hesitate to give God the glory for his new life and the blessings in it.

Tracing God's faithfulness to us down the years is probably the most encouraging thing we can do to fortify us for the future. As we recognise his kindness to us in the past, we learn to rely on it for all of our tomorrows. Even if, unlike Joseph, we are not always proud of the choices we have made in the past or feel that we have wobbled in our trust in God on many an occasion, God offers us forgiveness even before we ask for it. His grace far outstrips our shortcomings.

It is said that no matter what we do for God, we cannot outgive him. How are you aware of what God has given to you? Can you name and thank him for those things today?

DI ARCHER

Forgive and forget?

'Didn't I tell you not to sin against the boy?' Reuben asked. 'But you wouldn't listen. And now we have to answer for his blood!' Of course, they didn't know that Joseph understood them, for he had been speaking to them through an interpreter. Now he turned away from them and began to weep. (vv. 22–24, NLT)

Events took yet another dramatic turn for Joseph, as he recognised his brothers who had come to Egypt to buy food for the famine-stricken family. By this time, Joseph was selling stored grain to both Egyptians and foreigners. As his brothers bowed low before him, he must have recalled those long-ago dreams which had foreshadowed this very moment. But the wounds from his brothers' ill treatment of him were still there. Joseph was emotional, but extremely wary. Could he trust them? Did Reuben's words mean that the brothers really had changed and were sorry for what they had done? He had to test them to find out the truth.

To test their consciences, Joseph accused them of spying, grilled them as to their family news, held Simeon captive and ordered that the money due was surreptitiously returned. He also promised to let them live if they returned with Benjamin and gave them extra supplies for the journey.

High drama indeed. High emotions, too, on all sides. Joseph may well have forgiven his brothers before this occasion, but reconciliation was a completely different proposition. For all he knew, the brothers were still meting out violence and injustice. Forgiving others is no small task, especially when the hurt is big and deep. Reconciliation is only possible when both parties can begin again, and for some situations that is not an option. We may not hold those who have wounded us to account any more, but we would be most unwise to open ourselves to severe levels of abuse again. Neither would this help the perpetrator. Everyday forgiveness and making up in close relationships is important; creating appropriate boundaries where unreasonable hurt may be repeated is crucial. Do you know when to mend a relationship, and when it is best consigned to the past?

Read Matthew 18:21–35. How does forgiveness relate to justice?

DI ARCHER

Just desserts

The brothers were terrified when they saw that they were being taken into Joseph's house. 'It's because of the money someone put in our sacks last time we were here,' they said. 'He plans to pretend that we stole it. Then he will seize us, make us slaves, and take our donkeys.' (v. 18, NLT)

Joseph did a thorough job of frightening his brothers when they reluctantly returned to Egypt for more food. They were convinced he would condemn them as spies. But thankfully they *had* changed their ways – and readily owned up to the money they had found in their sacks. Joseph must have been somewhat reassured; but his tests were not over yet. He still did not consider it safe to reveal his true identity to them.

Forgiveness can take time, and reconciliation is often tiny step by tiny step. Joseph's behaviour shows how conflicted he was – rushing out to cry in private over seeing his brother Benjamin again one minute, holding himself back from telling them the truth about himself the next. Underneath, he wanted reunion desperately. He feasted with his brothers; he played a little with them, seating them in birth order and spoiling Benjamin.

This is how it goes with deep relationship damage. We may want to restore connections, but are afraid to do so, wary of further hurt. Joseph was protective of himself in his slow journey towards trusting his family of origin. He was surely right to be so. However, unlike Joseph, we now have the advantage of knowing Jesus and he changes the parameters. We do not have the luxury of judging others without bringing that same judgement on ourselves. Whatever crimes have been committed against us, we too need forgiveness. We too have sinned, and now live dependent on the grace of God. We see amazing examples of Christians reaching out in extreme circumstances to forgive those who caused them harm. While careful boundaries are important, the Holy Spirit living in us makes the most extraordinary acts of forgiveness and reconciliation possible.

What is the hardest thing you have had to forgive? Or are there wounds that still need to heal, and forgiveness you need to offer – whether in conversation with God or with another?

DI ARCHER

Judah steps up

'So please, my lord, let me stay here as a slave instead of the boy, and let the boy return with his brothers. For how can I return to my father if the boy is not with me? I couldn't bear to see the anguish this would cause my father!' (vv. 33–34, NLT)

Joseph still wasn't done testing his brothers. This time, when he sent them away, he repeated the returned money trick and added his own silver cup into Benjamin's sack. Then he caused them to be chased down and exposed. But this time, the brothers were desperate. They refused to allow Benjamin to be hiked off as Joseph's slave; they all returned to the palace and threw themselves on the floor before Joseph. Then came Judah's redeeming moment in the spotlight. He stepped up and spoke out, presumably not an easy thing to do within palace protocol. He explained the family history, the sadness of losing Joseph, and begged to be allowed to take Benjamin's place as slave, rather than risk their father Jacob's grief.

Thus, at last Joseph saw in one of his brothers the same resilience, courage and commitment to compassion and sacrifice that he knew to be in himself. Perhaps his blood ties had merit after all.

Joseph could still have chosen justified revenge, even now. His brothers' lives were in his hands, just as his had been in theirs. Was it even possible to heal such a traumatic past? What would he do? What do we do when the opportunity comes for mending fractured relationships? Are we able to rebuild or do we write others off permanently? Are others 'in' or 'out' with us, depending on their behaviour? Do we suck up prejudices from the news we read or popular opinions on social media, or do we try to find out more about the truth of situations? Joseph's decision would affect the history of Israel and, ultimately, our history. Who knows what repercussions will flow from the decisions you make regarding relationships. Take time, like Joseph, to consider, test and commit your decisions to God.

Read James 1:5. Dear Father, you see where decisions I make today may lead me and others. Please help me with every choice and keep my feet firmly walking next to yours. Amen.

DI ARCHER

The great reveal

'I am Joseph!' he said to his brothers. 'Is my father still alive?' But his brothers were speechless! They were stunned to realise that Joseph was standing there in front of them. 'Please, come closer,' he said to them… 'I am Joseph, your brother, whom you sold into slavery in Egypt.' (vv. 3–4, NLT)

Talk about drama! Joseph had had enough. He made his choice. Crying again, this time in a full meltdown, he invited his brothers close to him to tell them who he really was. What an incredible revelation! No wonder they were stunned. Did they, even in that extraordinary moment, suddenly remember the dreams that their little brother had told them, all those years ago? Did that memory prepare them for Joseph's faith-filled words, as he reassured them of his own understanding that God had worked all things together for their good (Romans 8:28)? That God had sent him ahead of them, to save their lives, now and throughout the coming years of famine?

As they hung back in shock, they must have taken some convincing. Perhaps Joseph took off his linen cloak and Egyptian regalia. His words tumbled over themselves as he invited the family to come and live in Egypt and promised he'd give them all they would need. But it was the hug that did it. Once he hugged Benjamin, the brothers really saw Joseph again.

What a wonderful moment. God had kept his word. He had rewarded Joseph's trust. He had worked through a dysfunctional family, a random caravan of traders, an influential guard captain, a vengeful woman, a perceptive prison warder, a forgetful cupbearer, a worried king and an international crisis. He fulfilled six mysterious dreams. He rescued Joseph's extended family and all their possessions. He blessed Joseph. He saved many lives, not just the Israelites'.

What would have happened to the story of our salvation, had Joseph not chosen to forgive? Had Jacob's sons all been wiped out by a bitter and proud naturalised Egyptian overlord? Had Jacob not moved to Egypt? God does know what he is doing.

Thank you, dear Father, that your perspective is so much bigger than mine. Please help me to trust you, rather than my own limited sight. Amen.

DI ARCHER

The long game

'I am God, the God of your father,' the voice said. 'Do not be afraid to go down to Egypt, for there I will make your family into a great nation. I will go with you down to Egypt, and I will bring you back again. You will die in Egypt, but Joseph will be with you to close your eyes.' (vv. 3–4, NLT)

Jacob and his entourage set off for Egypt in response to Joseph's invitation. He stopped at his old abode in Beersheba and offered sacrifices in worship to God. That night, God encouraged Jacob in a vision, reassuring him in specific terms that moving to Egypt was a good thing and that he was with him in it. He also renewed his promise that he would make Jacob's family into a great nation. Bearing in mind that there were only 70 people in Jacob's family, plus women and servants, that was quite a promise.

Perhaps it was easier for Jacob to believe this promise since the glorious reappearance of Joseph in his life. Jacob was full of thankfulness for this (v. 30). There's nothing like seeing God at work to lift spirits and faith. Joseph was an emotional heap – again – when he and his father were finally reunited, clinging to him for 'a long time' (v. 29). Having not seen each other for 22 long years, perhaps they both recognised in a new way that God seems to play the long game. Neither of them could have predicted their amazing reunion. Neither of them could have guessed that it would be in Egypt that their family would grow and multiply into a great nation.

This was due in large part to another good decision Joseph made. Recognising the unpopularity of Semitic shepherds like his family in Egypt, Joseph shrewdly recommended that they request to settle in Goshen, which offered rich pasture. Not only did this enable the new arrivals to thrive, but it also kept them separate from the Egyptians in general. So rather than be assimilated into Egyptian society, Jacob's family had the space and resources to grow into the great nation God had promised they would. The long game.

How very special that Jacob paused on his journey to Egypt to worship God and mark the occasion. How do you show your gratitude to God? Today is a good day to pause and do so.

DI ARCHER

Against the tide

'You have saved our lives!' they exclaimed. 'May it please you, my lord, to let us be Pharaoh's servants.' Joseph then issued a decree still in effect in the land of Egypt, that Pharaoh should receive one-fifth of all the crops grown on his land. (vv. 25–26, NLT)

While Joseph's understanding of God's long game in his life included saving the lives of his extended family, there was more to it than that, for all of Egypt was rescued by his wisdom and foresight in storing grain. The whole population was reduced to servitude in return for food and sustenance, a situation which they seem to have embraced willingly. The biblical explanation for this is that Egypt was blessed because it welcomed Abraham's descendants (Genesis 12:2–3), and here Jacob blessed Pharoah in turn. Joseph was a benign leader on behalf of Pharoah, averting a national disaster. There surely were those around him in the years of fruitful harvests who questioned his actions in storing up so much grain. But Joseph had a solid belief in God's guidance through dreams and got on with the job.

How are you at resisting negativity around you, or discouragement from others? There is always plenty around us to pull us away from trusting God and his word. In these days of multiple access points to news, views and opinions, the world is a very noisy place. The global marketplace can be a harsh environment. Even entertainment can subtly undermine our worldview, assuming a godless universe rather than a created world in which a loving God invites us to connect with him.

Like Joseph, we would do well to keep our eyes firmly on what we know is right to do, especially at those times when we are called to specific tasks, ministries or serving opportunities. This can take some doing but being resolute in bringing our thoughts and feelings to God every day, and submitting them to him, makes so much difference. If we do, we are so much more likely to experience his peace, be comforted by his presence and be challenged where necessary. We follow the one who made prayer a priority, so let's find ways to do the same.

Read Zephaniah 3:17. Dear Father, help me to enjoy you enjoying me! Amen.

DI ARCHER

Joseph and that verse

But Joseph replied, 'Don't be afraid of me. Am I God, that I can punish you? You intended to harm me, but God intended it all for good. He brought me to this position so I could save the lives of many people.' (vv. 19–20, NLT)

Despite all the reconciliation that had happened between Joseph and his brothers since they moved to Egypt, when their father Jacob died, they were afraid that Joseph might not stay his hand against them. They threw themselves on his mercy, offering to be slaves, which reduced Joseph to tears for the hundredth time. What a gloriously emotional man! However, thank goodness the brothers did this. Otherwise, we would not have Joseph's response. His words have held countless numbers of God-followers steady in days of crisis and challenge. They are the pinnacle of the whole Joseph story.

You may well have held on to this principle yourself. I know I have, more than once. Through Joseph's declaration, we see that God can use the difficult things in our lives for good. Others may hurt us, but God can weave the most amazing goodness out of the most dreadful circumstances and events. He can turn our most awful trials into sources of strength. Those who wish us harm never have the last word. Even should we lose our lives, we are still safe in the everlasting arms of our heavenly Father.

In my work with the charity *Tastelifeuk* and seeing the struggles of those with eating disorders as they battle to walk out of them and back into life, I have seen this process again and again. In prison, just as surely as Joseph was, they too learn incredible staying power, determination, self-knowledge and eventual freedom. Many of us would echo their words as they testify to harm being absorbed by good in their lives, giving them previously unimagined strength. God can take anything and weave it for our benefit. Bad things are still bad, but they are not beyond God's gracious kindness. He plays the long game.

We may have plans, but God has a purpose. He worked out this purpose throughout Joseph's life. He is doing the same with yours. Will you trust him?

DI ARCHER

God of the wind and rain

Sara Batts-Neale writes:

'Singin' in the rain' or 'Bring me sunshine' – which song sums up your attitude to the weather? I'm the owner of a dog who definitely needs a decent daily walk, so I've got used to going out in all sorts of conditions. I take to heart the maxim that 'there's no such thing as bad weather, just the wrong clothes', and I'm often so very thankful for the inventors of waterproof coats and wellington boots. Equally, I'm always pleased when there's sunshine, even if it's chilly. January's weather can be so unpredictable, can't it? I wonder what the weather is like as you're reading this, wherever you are. I'm based in England and so this time of year is sometimes snowy, sometimes cold. Oftentimes, it's just a bit wet and grey as we patiently wait for the days to slowly lengthen and the sun to reappear.

The science of weather forecasting is complex and fascinating. Did you know the UK's Met Office computers do 14,000 trillion calculations per second? Per second! I had to read that twice to fully understand that I couldn't understand that kind of computing capacity. It's mind-boggling. These supercomputers have enabled predictions to become increasingly accurate during my living memory. Meteorologists can predict the rainbow, the jet stream or the thunderstorm that allows us to plan our lives tomorrow and warn us of the dangers of climate change in years ahead.

Knowing the science behind how a rainbow is formed doesn't detract from its beauty – or stop it being a powerful symbol of hope. Predicting the arrival of spring rain doesn't make the raindrops less refreshing and life-giving. The intensity of a thunderstorm is not lessened by understanding what causes lightning. Over the next few days, we will find biblical explanations and metaphors for the weather. We'll sit alongside Job as God answers him out of the whirlwind; read about rain in the Song of Solomon and Hosea; think about clouds, rain and a little bit of sunshine. We're going to think about weather as a starting point to reflect on God's power and sovereignty, on his beautiful creation, on our blessings and on our lives lived with him.

Lightning flashes of inspiration

The crash of your thunder was in the whirlwind; your lightnings lit up the world; the earth trembled and shook. (v. 18, NRSV)

How do you feel about thunderstorms? A few years ago, I was visiting friends in Cambodia. As we drove across the country, one night we travelled through an enthralling display of lightning in the night sky, vastly different from anything I'd ever seen before. It was beautiful, even though I was anxious. I do dislike the oppressive atmosphere that can precede a big storm. I find it hard to concentrate and end up with a niggling headache. The storm itself is often a real release – I watch the rain and hear the thunder with a sense of gratefulness that something has passed.

I wonder if that's what's going on for our psalmist today. The first few verses certainly tell of trouble, don't they? A sense of abandonment by God, of sleepless nights searching for answers while beset by memories of earlier, better times. The psalmist is in despair. Yet, this is a psalm of two halves, and the mood changes in verse 10 as the psalmist deliberately turns from sorrowful thoughts. Suddenly the psalmist is inspired to praise God. Remembering the days of old becomes a thing of joy, not of torment, as God's past deeds are recalled and meditated on. The power of God is extolled through the stormy imagery. Crashing thunder and flashing arrows of lightning so terrific that the very seas are afraid. What an awesome God this is!

We'll see on Saturday that storms are often seen as a sign of God's presence. In recalling an image of a powerful storm, the psalmist finds their peace. They remember that God is powerful, and God leads us even if we cannot see his footprints on the way ahead.

'The voice of the Lord is over the waters; the God of glory thunders, the Lord thunders over the mighty waters' (Psalm 29:3, NIV).

SARA BATTS-NEALE

Cloudy thinking

Praise the Lord! How good it is to sing praises to our God; for he is gracious, and a song of praise is fitting. (v. 1, NRSV)

Are you a daydreamer? I'm writing this on a chilly, overcast morning, and my thoughts are wandering off to warm days, blue skies and time to sit watching fluffy white clouds drifting by. I am always pleasantly surprised when other people can also see the same rabbit or mountain or ghost or whatever it is that I've decided is there in the formation!

I know about different types of cloud and how they form, and what kind of weather they predict. That doesn't stop me taking delight in the idea that they're God's handiwork; the same delight that our psalmist expresses today in something as simple as God covering the sky with clouds. It's partly the same sentiment as yesterday, words of restoration and of joy. When the psalmists want to praise, they really go all out, don't they? Psalm 147 paints such a glorious picture of a God in control. Our God who orders the heavens and earth to the benefit of his people. Our God who powerfully controls and directs the weather around us.

The same power that directs the snow, frost and hail also powerfully declares statutes and ordinances. The privilege of being God's chosen people is made clear. That's a privilege we now enjoy as God's children. We have hope because of his steadfast love – a hope of healing, of justice, of power.

This psalm also serves as a reminder of how things could be. After all, we know that sometimes rain doesn't fall where it's wanted – that there isn't always peace, or finest wheat. It is a psalm that gives us hope and reminds us that God can and will act. He is indeed to be praised!

Heavenly Father, we praise you for your wonderful works. You are sovereign over all. Help us to listen to your commands and follow your word in all we do today. Amen.

SARA BATTS-NEALE

Extravagant and beautiful creation

'Have you commanded the morning since your days began, and caused the dawn to know its place, so that it might take hold of the skirts of the earth, and the wicked be shaken out of it?' (vv. 12–13, NRSV)

On Sunday, we saw weather imagery used as a way of praising God. Today, we hear God himself telling of his greatness using creation as his starting point. Job really does have the patience of – well – Job! He's endured a lot at the hands of his friends. We are dipping into Job today just after Elihu's attempt to tell Job just how wrong Job is and how right God is. Finally, God responds out of the whirlwind. In no uncertain terms, God reminds us how foolish and ignorant we are besides God's handiwork and knowledge of his own creation.

I find such beauty in this language. The storehouse of snow or the dawn shaking out the skirts of the earth; the tilting of the waterskins of heaven. This isn't just a list of dry rhetorical questions – this is an exploration of the living, breathing purposes of God's creation, his sovereignty and his power. Poetry and images can really help us understand more about the extravagance and detail of the world we inhabit. We know the science – we know the *how* of how things happen. The Met Office can tell us when it's going to snow and discuss the formation of ice crystals into snowflakes. Yet in today's passage we have a glimpse of the *why*, God's mind behind the science. There is extravagance in God's creation. Did snowflakes need to be so intricate and varied? The infinite variety reflects a God who has no need to put limits on his handiwork. Abundant beauty in nature points us back to a God who is wonderfully extravagant. I wonder which weather image sits most powerfully with you from today's reading.

Maybe you find the glory of God not in a beautiful sunset but in the pounding of the rain. Whatever the weather today, let's look for God's handiwork around us.

SARA BATTS-NEALE

Rain as blessing

Get up, my dear friend, fair and beautiful lover – come to me!
Look around you: Winter is over; the winter rains are over, gone!
(vv. 10–11, MSG)

We moved into our current house when it was August. We tackled the over-long grass and the well-established weeds straight away, which left me musing upon why God thought bindweed was a good idea. We then had to wait and see what would happen as the seasons changed. I'm such a fan of spring flowers that I was rather disappointed when only one patch of narcissi appeared. It was a top priority for me to get bulbs in the ground in our second autumn. I look forward to cheery daffodils at this time of year. Spring is coming, and the world will be reborn again. The winter is past, the rain is over and gone. There is hope of new life, of new birth, of the greening of the trees.

Rain is necessary to help this abundance of new life grow. Rain is a blessing. It might not always feel like it, when our outdoors plans are postponed or our homes flooded. A life lived in Britain means that for me rain is something I rather assume just happens. As climate change accelerates, there are places around the world where rains are increasingly failing, and life is becoming more precarious as a result. If I take rain for granted, do I all too easily take other blessings for granted? Am I aware enough of the ways in which I'm blessed by God – the tiny, everyday things? Rain arrives in many forms – the kind of downpour that drenches in seconds as well as nuisance-value drizzle that seeps through seams. And so does our awareness of God in our lives! God's work is often noticed gradually, as life shifts slowly. It's not always an instant revelation.

Today, when you turn on a tap, thank God for all that is mundane. There are so many ways we are blessed in the ordinary moments and things of life around us. Let's try to notice them with gratitude.

SARA BATTS-NEALE

Prophesies of rain

Let us acknowledge the Lord; let us press on to acknowledge him. As surely as the sun rises, he will appear. (v. 3, NIV)

Yesterday, I took you into my garden to think about the passing of winter and spring blessings. Today, we're also thinking ahead with more spring rains. Hosea is one of the twelve minor prophets, and his book is full of speeches which are critical of the lives lived around him. Yesterday was a tale of love. Today, Hosea tells a tale of betrayal of the covenant made between God and his people. It's full of metaphors and it also describes Hosea's lived experience. Both show the relationship between Israel and the Lord completely in tatters.

Prophets offer hope – and today's passage is a call to repentance. Hosea points to the coming disaster (the overrunning of Israel by the Assyrians and resulting exile) as a punishment and consequence for Israel's rejection of the covenant and relationship with God.

Hosea is speaking to a whole community, not an individual. There's a sense of parched abandonment – a people in need of reviving, to whom the Lord will return. If we are far from God, and we return to him, we can be sure he will be with us. The trust we can place in God is as sure as the appearing of the dawn. He will come like the welcome spring showers that water the earth. When nature is getting ready to burst forth in spring, rain is nothing but a blessing. Rain quenches a dry and thirsty land. Young plants stretch out their roots to draw water. The presence of God, and knowledge of his forgiveness and of his love, refresh us. It's a challenge in our busy lives to stay connected, to not be distracted by the demands of our responsibilities, but if we press on to know the Lord, then he'll be there. Just as sure as the sun coming up tomorrow.

'For I will pour water on the thirsty land, and streams on the dry ground; I will pour out my spirit on your offspring, and my blessing on your descendants' (Isaiah 44:3).

SARA BATTS-NEALE

No small tempest

We were being pounded by the storm so violently that on the next day they began to throw the cargo overboard, and on the third day with their own hands they threw the ship's tackle overboard. When neither sun nor stars appeared for many days, and no small tempest raged, all hope of our being saved was at last abandoned. (vv. 18–20, NRSV)

This past summer I joined a local rowing club, with a boat called a pilot gig. This kind of boat would race out to an incoming vessel, because the first pilot to her would win the job (the gig) of bringing her safely into port. Shipwrecks are, after all, not a good thing. The winter winds are the cause of Paul's shipwreck, sailing in dangerous months where other vessels stayed in port.

Acts 27 narrates the journey from Caesarea to Rome. Paul had appealed to the Roman Emperor in the face of continued threats. The voyage was full of tension and fear. 'No small tempest' (v. 20) rages around them as the crew throws cargo overboard. The ship is driven by violent winds. And amid all this – in the midst of a crew thinking only of escape, with no hope for the ship – Paul speaks words of calm and thanksgiving. He shares a vision in which an angel declared God had granted all the crew safety. I'd love to have been a fly on the wall to hear the sailors' reactions to this pronouncement! That's not recorded, of course. What is written, though, is that Paul took bread, gave thanks to God, broke it and ate it – the actions that are familiar now from our Eucharist or Holy Communion. In my church tradition the Eucharist is central. Food for the journey. Just as it is for Paul in Acts, so it is for us, particularly when we are navigating the storms of life. It's interesting to me that there's a shipwreck coming. For that might not be our favoured outcome of a rocky moment in life. Yet Paul has trust in God; he thanks God in the midst of a storm. Whatever life is throwing at us, we can do the same.

What are the storms you're weathering right now? Can you find a moment today to stop and give thanks to God, in the midst of all the turmoil?

SARA BATTS-NEALE

Atmospheric apocalypse

There were loud voices in heaven, saying, 'The kingdom of the world has become the kingdom of our Lord and of his Messiah, and he will reign forever and ever.' (v. 15, NRSV)

The first time I encountered the book of Revelation I was bemused. It felt like a collection of ideas that were impossible to imagine, interspersed with words that are familiar from liturgy and song. A contrast between the familiar and the strange, yet both helping to illustrate the vision for the apocalypse. Apocalypse is a word that means 'uncovering'.

In today's passage, we read of the ark of the covenant being revealed as God's temple in heaven was opened. The ark was the holiest of holies – resting in the tabernacle and in the temple, behind a curtain, visited only by the priests. This curtain was torn in two at the moment Jesus died on the cross (Matthew 27:50–51), which speaks to me of a positive ability for us to find a way to God through Christ. Here the ark is seen as judgement on the nations begins. The revealing of the ark is accompanied by the storm of all storms – lightning, hail and peals of thunder. If this passage was being dramatised as a play, this weather would be literally atmospheric. It is showing us the importance of the words of the elders, showing us the depth and seriousness of God's judgement on those who have not revered his name. In a sense, I think that's the essence of living as a Christian – to revere God's name isn't just not using it as a swear word but worshipping God's whole authority. St Augustine said, 'Love God and do whatever you please: for the soul trained in love to God will do nothing to offend the One who is Beloved.' When we love God, we find ourselves drawn into a way of life that serves him and brings the kingdom of our Lord closer to the kingdom of the world.

Merciful God, I want to live a life not of fear of judgement but in joyful worship. I want to live a life that builds your kingdom and shows how you reign. Amen.

SARA BATTS-NEALE

The letters of John

Rosemary Green writes:

Unlike most New Testament letters, 1 John does not tell us who wrote it. But many signs point in the same direction, that it was written by the disciple John, towards the end of the first century. Similarities of language to John's gospel; the eyewitness testimony and the indications of a close relationship with the Lord; the authoritative tone that would come from an apostle; the suggestion of the author's old age; the leading theologians in the second century – Irenaeus, Clement of Alexandria, Tertullian and Origen – all affirm that the author was the apostle, John. Even the strong description of the heretics as antichrists, liars and children of the devil reminds us that Jesus called John and his brother James 'sons of thunder' (Mark 3:17, NIV) – though John is better known as the apostle of love. We meet him in the gospels from the earliest days of Jesus' ministry, alongside James and Peter, the inner trio of Jesus' closest friends.

The letter has no references to any individuals and probably went to many churches in the area round Ephesus (in modern western Turkey), where John was living. Its main thrust was to counter the start of Gnosticism, one of the most dangerous heresies in the early church. The Gnosticism addressed by John was an early form of the heresy, not the intricate system that developed later. Its central teaching was that the spirit is entirely good, and matter – including the human body – entirely evil. Several falsehoods flowed from this unbiblical idea, and the Gnostics were convinced that their special knowledge made them superior to all other Christians. Their misconceptions led them to deny Christ's incarnation (some said that Christ only seemed to have a body; others that the divine Christ joined with the man Jesus at baptism and left him before he died). They also believed that since it was matter itself that was evil, breaking God's law through our bodies was of no moral consequence, and thus all bodily moral restraints were rejected. So John's two basic purposes in writing were to expose the false teachers and to help believers to be sure of their faith; 'that you may know' is a key, repeated phrase in the letter.

We will spend the majority of our time over the next two weeks studying this first letter and then consider 2 and 3 John, which are much shorter and were written to specific people.

We knew him!

That which was from the beginning, which we have heard, which we have seen with our eyes, which we have looked at and our hands have touched – this we proclaim concerning the Word of life. (v. 1, NIV)

I love the assurance with which John opens his letter! As we saw in the introduction, there was a group of Christians (who later developed as the second-century Gnostics) who deserted the church. They clung to the teaching that all flesh is corrupt; only the soul is pure. So they denied that Jesus could possibly be God come in the flesh. John counteracts this in no uncertain terms. He writes, in effect, 'I was there. We saw him, we touched him, we heard him. We are first-hand witnesses.'

Personal experience assured John that Jesus was God incarnate, God in bodily human form. He wanted his readers to be sure of it too, so that they might share in the fellowship that he enjoyed with God the Father and God the Son.

He wants us to be equally sure. The foundation of our faith in Christ is mind-boggling: the infinite, eternal God born as a vulnerable baby. As we ponder that near-impossible fact – the infinite God who came as a tiny infant – we could be tempted to say, 'That can't be true!' Concurrently, that utterly astonishing truth can become so familiar that we become almost blasé about it and lose our wonder.

I grew up in a church-going home. A non-questioning child, I took for granted the virgin birth, Jesus' miracles, his death and resurrection as historical facts. It was, however, ancient history and made little impact on my life – until I saw that I wasn't the goody-goody I thought I was. I was like a shiny red apple; one blemish on the outside, black and maggoty inside. Jesus' death bought the forgiveness I needed, and his resurrection meant that he was alive to be my friend. Jesus was indeed God come as human, who became my living Saviour.

Lord, thank you for John's first-hand experience of the amazing truth that you came in the flesh. Thank you even more that you want to be the core of our lives. Amen.

ROSEMARY GREEN

Walk in the light

God is light; in him there is no darkness at all. If we claim to have fellowship with him and yet walk in the darkness, we lie and do not live out the truth. (vv. 5a–6, NIV)

John seems to set an impossible standard for us! 'God is light.' His holiness is like a white sheet of paper, without a single mark to spoil its purity. As Habakkuk put it seven centuries before John wrote, 'Your eyes are too pure to look on evil; you cannot tolerate wrongdoing' (1:13). It is hard for us, in our varying shades of grey, even to imagine how pure, how holy, is that God of light who detests sin.

Yet John tells his readers to walk in the light, in the light of God's holiness. How can we get anywhere near him? 1:7 shows us: 'The blood of Jesus, his Son, purifies us from all sin.' I have known that and sought to live by it for over 70 years. Yet I have still not fully grasped the enormity of what Jesus did for us on the cross: 'He is the atoning sacrifice for our sins, and not only for ours but also for the sins of the whole world' (2:2). My mind boggles at its hugeness, and at the generosity of his love.

However, no matter how clear I am that Jesus' death covers every petty wrongdoing, guilt can keep sneaking up, whether over a 'big' sin or something comparably trivial. In those moments, I turn 1:9 into a personal prayer: 'If I confess my sin, you, God, are faithful and just and will forgive me my sin and purify me from all unrighteousness.' His forgiveness does not depend on me. It rests on his character of faithfulness and justice. If I don't let him convince me that he can and does forgive me, I am doubting his character.

Perhaps, to complete my assurance that I am forgiven, I need to confess my wrongdoing to another person. That can be harder! God already knows my worst; the other person doesn't, and I cannot be sure how he or she will accept my admission. Their reaction, however, is their responsibility, not mine.

We do not need to evade admission of wrongdoing to have a clear conscience. We might pray: 'Lord, thank you that you want me to be sure that you forgive me. Please give me that assurance deep down. Amen.'

ROSEMARY GREEN

God's love in us

We know that we have come to know him if we keep his commands. Whoever says, 'I know him,' but does not do what he commands is a liar, and the truth is not in that person. But if anyone obeys his word, love for God is truly made complete in them. (vv. 3–5, NIV)

Years of caring for a young family, plus resentment against my husband's freedom to travel, drained my spiritual vitality. I realised that I knew little about loving people, and I would pray with gritted teeth, 'Please give me that love.' One hand was open, but my other hand was clenched tight: 'No, it would be too costly.' I was stuck, until a stressful situation made me, independent though I was, accept the loving help being offered. I let down my barriers to people; God's love flowed from them to me and was planted in me. His Spirit flowed in to revive me, and I was free to love other people with God's love. A few weeks later, I flew to South Africa to join my husband, convalescing from meningitis. I told him two things: 'I've learnt the value of a hug' and 'I've begun to say, "I love Jesus."' Love for God and love for people go hand in hand.

John's emphasis today is on the obedience to God that enables his love to flow out of us. He is clear. If we live in God's light and love, we will love others in the Christian family. Light and love are partners; so are darkness and hatred. I think with shame of the Christians I sometimes try to avoid. It is obviously not going to be easy to love everyone, but we can ask God to give us his quality of love, even for those we find unlovable. I know he can do it; he has done it for me.

Verse 7 takes us straight back to Jesus, when he said to his disciples, 'A new command I give you: love one another. As I have loved you, so you must love one another' (John 13:34). That would mark them as his followers.

Father, please open my heart to embrace the wonder of your love – your love for me, and the love you can give me to love unlovely people. Thank you for Jesus' cross, the hard evidence of your love. Amen.

ROSEMARY GREEN

Why John wrote

I write to you, dear children, because you know the Father. I write to you, fathers, because you know him who is from the beginning. I write to you, young men, because you are strong, and the word of God lives in you, and you have overcome the evil one. (v. 14, NIV)

One of the things that annoys my offspring is my frequent repetition. I sometimes wonder if the old man John was doing the same thing – though I reckon he had all his marbles and was right in tune with God. His repetition emphasises what he thought most important: knowing the Father, overcoming evil and trusting in the word of God – all vital in our lives.

This letter is full of John's desire for us to know – both to know God in relationship, and to know the truth about him. He wanted his readers to stay firm in God's truth, not be deflected by the damaging twists that were creeping in. Remember that much of the New Testament had been written down before John was writing and would already have been circulating round the churches.

There is a strong link between the phrases 'you are strong', 'the word of God lives in you' and 'you have overcome the evil one'. How did Jesus overcome the devil's temptations in the wilderness? He was strong in his counterattack with words from the Old Testament. Learning verses from the Bible by heart is less fashionable than it was when I was younger; but it still gives us tools to use when we are discouraged or tempted to go off track in our thinking or our behaviour.

What are the heresies you see pervading our current society? There is no plumb line of an absolute truth: 'Your truth is what you believe, and my truth is what I believe.' One example might be the expectation of many bereaved people to be reunited with their departed loved ones, despite no belief in Jesus or his resurrection.

Lord, I am surrounded by many conflicting attitudes that ignore you and your ways. Please help me to discern your truth. Amen.

ROSEMARY GREEN

Stand firm

As for you, see that what you have heard from the beginning remains in you. If it does, you also will remain in the Son and in the Father… I am writing these things to you about those who are trying to lead you astray. (v. 24 and v. 26, NIV)

We have read some long and slightly convoluted verses today. So, expect some hard work in unpacking and understanding what John is saying! He opened this letter with the affirmation that Jesus really was God in human form. He continues now to show his deep concern about the false teaching of those who had left the church, and that those who were stuck might be lured away by their lies (v. 26). 'Who is the liar? It is whoever denies that Jesus is the Christ' (v. 22). 'Antichrist', he calls them; that is a pretty strong description!

I think John had in mind the warnings Jesus gave them in the last week of his life, as he replied to his disciples' questions about the signs of the end of the age; warnings like, 'Watch out that no one deceives you. For many will come in my name, claiming, "I am the Messiah", and will deceive many' (Matthew 24:4–5). John's awareness of the false teachers seems to have reinforced his expectation that Jesus' return was imminent. If John (and Peter likewise, 1 Peter 4:7) had their timing wrong, we make the opposite mistake. Two thousand years later, he hasn't come yet, and most of us ignore Jesus' second coming altogether. Jesus said he might come at any time and his followers should be ready (Matthew 24:42–44).

Alongside his warnings, John wants to encourage his fellow Christians. What he is saying, in effect, is, 'Stay true to what you believe; then you will remain close to God' (v. 24). What does he mean by 'an anointing' (v. 20)? More of John's memories from Jesus' teaching at the end of his life. 'When he, the Spirit of truth, comes, he will guide you into all the truth' (John 16:13).

Reflect on the Bible teaching you have been given. Then think about the subtle (or not so subtle) words and influences that could deflect you from the truths you know.

ROSEMARY GREEN

Love and purity

See what great love the Father has lavished on us, that we should be called children of God! And that is what we are! The reason the world does not know us is that it did not know him. (v. 1, NIV)

Do you know a family with an adopted child? The parents pour as much love on that child as any biological offspring they may have; the child is as much part of the family as any other children. That is our position when we are adopted into God's family. Many people think that we are all children of God. I'm afraid they are mistaken. We are all his creation, but we are not all his children. John 1:12 makes that clear: 'To all who did receive him, to those who believed in his name, he gave the right to become children of God.' It gives extra richness to John's words in verse 1: 'See what great love the Father has lavished on us, that we should be called children of God!' Wow! John really wants us to rejoice in God's lavish love. Many Christians are not sure, deep down, of that love. For many years as a Christian, I sought to know the reality of that love. I prayed about it. I talked with a wise Christian counsellor. Still that confidence eluded me, until something apparently small and insignificant enabled me to say, 'Now I have felt that love.' I can't even remember what happened. Yet it left me with a kernel of assurance. God loves me.

Privilege, however, goes hand in hand with responsibility. That is the focus of verses 3–10. 'No one who is born of God will continue to sin, because God's seed remains in them' (v. 9). When we have received Christ's Spirit into our being and have become God's child, our new nature shows itself in new behaviour. John is not expecting sinless perfection, but he does expect our new nature as a child of God to be seen in a new victory over habitual sin.

Reread verses 1–10 slowly, aloud if possible. Write down the words that most challenge you. Then pray that verse 3 may become real in you, that you may willingly collaborate with the resident Holy Spirit in purifying you.

ROSEMARY GREEN

Love in practice

This is how we know what love is: Jesus Christ laid down his life for us. And we ought to lay down our lives for our brothers and sisters. (v. 16, NIV)

Love is no mere wishy-washy feeling. Love is concerned for the other person; love is practical; love is costly; love must be seen to be real. So, John expresses how we see hard evidence of love in action.

First, he reminds us of the solid evidence we have of God's love for us. His love is expressed in many ways, but the supreme mark of his love is seen in Jesus' death on the cross. That love was not short-term, seen only as Jesus wrestled in prayer in Gethsemane or as he hung on the cross for six hours during his execution. His love is eternal. The God who created the world, who created humankind and saw that 'it was very good' (Genesis 1:31) knew that we would go astray and spoil his good world. Jesus is described as 'the Lamb who was slain from the creation of the world' (Revelation 13:8). Paul writes equally clearly: 'God demonstrates his own love for us in this: while we were still sinners, Christ died for us' (Romans 5:8). We must never brush over the depth of God's love for us, seen supremely in Jesus' death for us.

Second, John looks for hard evidence of our love for one another. 'Dear children, let us not love with words or speech but with actions and in truth' (v. 18). Verse 16 tells us that our love for one another should be of the same quality as God's love for us. That's pretty challenging! If God's love is real in us that will lead to action. Maybe there is a local food bank you could give to, or an international aid organisation you could donate to regularly? Could you buy a sandwich for the next homeless person you walk past rather than just putting your head down and scurring by? Precisely what love in practice looks like will vary, but in both small and bigger ways we are called to love 'with actions and in truth'.

God, thank you for the immensity of your love for me. Please show me how to express my thanks in the way I show your love to others in my individual circumstances. Amen.

ROSEMARY GREEN

Inner security

My dear children, let's not just talk about love; let's practice real love. This is the only way we'll know we're living truly, living in God's reality. It's also the way to shut down debilitating self-criticism, even when there is something to it. For God is greater than our worried hearts. (vv. 18–20, MSG)

Do you feel secure in your relationship with God? John wants us to be really sure of our faith – knowing the truth in our heads and knowing God in our hearts. That word 'security' is not spelled out in today's verses, but the intertwining of knowing, belonging and keeping his commands communicates it. It's the security of a child who knows that she is loved by her daddy, of a boy who can jump off a high wall and know that daddy will catch him. It is the security of a girl who can whisper secrets to mummy and know she will not be betrayed. It's the security of a child who knows that 'I forgive you' doesn't mean, 'I'll remind you of that mistake, many times.'

Sadly, many of us have not known that sort of parental security in childhood. That makes it hard (though not impossible) to know that security in adult relationship with our heavenly Father. My father died when I was a baby, and I never knew what it meant to have an earthly father. The thought that God knows everything (v. 20) was scary. I felt vulnerable knowing that God, the judge, knew all my sins and secrets. Then I learned, deep down, that he really is my heavenly Father who knows the worst about me yet loves me just the same. I am very grateful for that assurance that gave me a new sense of inner security.

Look at the last sentence in today's verses. 'And this is how we know that he lives in us: we know it by the Spirit he gave us' (NIV). It is God's Holy Spirit, resident in each one of us who has invited him into our lives, who can change us and make us sure of our relationship with God.

'You have searched me, Lord, and you know me. You know when I sit and when I rise; you perceive my thoughts from afar… Such knowledge is too wonderful for me.' Read Psalm 139:1–10 and let its words seep into you.

ROSEMARY GREEN

Recognising the truth

This is how you can recognise the Spirit of God: every spirit that acknowledges that Jesus Christ has come in the flesh is from God, but every spirit that does not acknowledge Jesus is not from God… This is how we recognise the Spirit of truth and the spirit of falsehood. (vv. 2–3 and v. 6, NIV)

Read the same verses 2–3 in the modern *The Message* translation: 'Here's how you test for the genuine Spirit of God. Everyone who confesses openly his faith in Jesus Christ – the Son of God, who came as an actual flesh-and-blood person – comes from God and belongs to God. And everyone who refuses to confess faith in Jesus has nothing in common with God'.

Our society has a flexible attitude to truth, with no measure for an absolute truth; people present an argument from their perspective and assume it is as good as anyone else's ('whoever is not from God does not listen to us', v. 6). John knew how easily his readers were led astray and he wanted them to have a rock-solid test for truth; he rests that on the incarnation of Jesus (remember that was the prime error in his day).

What an encouragement this phrase from verse 4 is, especially when we are struggling with some chronic temptation: 'The one who is in you is greater than the one who is in the world.' That 'one who is in us' is God's Holy Spirit, the Spirit of truth. When Paul prayed for the Ephesian church, he asked that they might know 'his incomparably great power for us who believe. That power is the same as the mighty strength he exerted when he raised Christ from the dead' (Ephesians 1:19–20). That bowled me over when I first read it. The same power that raised Jesus from the dead resides in us.

Lord, thank you for your Holy Spirit living in me. Thank you that he is called the Spirit of truth, and that he can guide me to know your truth. Amen.

ROSEMARY GREEN

Love is number one

Everyone who loves has been born of God and knows God. Whoever does not love does not know God, because God is love. This is how God showed his love among us: he sent his one and only Son into the world that we might live through him. (vv. 7–10, NIV)

These verses are permeated with love – God's self-sacrificial love, which he expects to see reproduced in us. As you look at people around you, how many of them do you think put themselves as number one in their lives? My rights, my job, my family, my success. Do you react, 'Surely, that's not me!'? But when the budget is announced, what do I notice? My first thought is more likely to be, 'How is that going to affect me?' rather than, 'Will that be good for the nation?' How different that attitude is from the theme of today's verses, with their focus on love – God's love; his love that should permeate our whole being, in character, thought and behaviour.

Love puts the other person first. I think the main characteristic of love is that it always wants the best for the other person, even at its own expense. That is seen supremely in Jesus' death on the cross. God sets the standard high, and he looks for such self-sacrificial love in us.

I like to think that love rules me. Yet as I currently look out from my front room on the gas board's ugly fencing to facilitate the work they are doing to renew old pipes, I am more concerned for the way it spoils my usual pleasant view than I am about the danger it causes traffic. That is not an attitude of love.

'He has given us this command: anyone who loves God must also love their brother and sister' (v. 21) – that includes the brother and sister in our nuclear or church family. This morning I was at a church coffee morning and instead of going to sit with the sad-looking stranger on his own, I stayed with my friends. Mine was not the action of love.

I hoped to show how my love today had made the invisible God a bit more visible, but I am disappointed in myself. What about you? Lord, please transform me with your love, so that I may truly demonstrate what you are like. Amen.
ROSEMARY GREEN

Faith in the incarnation

And this is the testimony: God has given us eternal life, and this life is in his Son. Whoever has the Son has life; whoever does not have the Son of God does not have life. (vv. 11–12, NIV)

Sometimes we are given a plate of food that looks pretty indigestible. Perhaps we just eat the bits that look most attractive before we tackle any of the rest. Today's verses are rather like that! So let's focus on the last two verses. We see a cause for rejoicing, and a cause for concern. We rejoice in the assurance of eternal life through Jesus. Eternal life is not just life that lasts forever; we don't know exactly what that life will be like, but we know it will be glorious to see Jesus face-to-face. We even get a glimpse of its quality while we live on earth (just dimly, as Paul tells us in 1 Corinthians 13:12). 'Whoever has the Son has life' – John wants us to live in the light of that assurance. The flip side is the tough side of the gospel, the concern we should have for friends and family who do not know him on this earth and who will be without him for eternity.

Verses 1–5 return to the themes of faith, obedience and love. John had not forgotten Jesus' words at the last supper: 'My command is this: love each other as I have loved you' (John 15:12).

Verses 6–9 are perplexing, and scholars do not all agree. It seems that John was counteracting the heretical Gnostics who denied that at his baptism (reference to water) and death (reference to blood) Jesus was fully divine. As the Living Bible puts it, 'So we have these three witnesses: the voice of the Holy Spirit in our hearts, the voice from heaven at Christ's baptism, and the voice before he died. And they all say the same thing: that Jesus Christ is the Son of God' (vv. 7–8).

Lord, some parts of the Bible are hard to understand. Please help me to live in the light of truths that are clear. I want to live life to the full (John 10:10), walking with you in love and obedience. Amen.

ROSEMARY GREEN

Confidence

My purpose in writing is simply this: that you who believe in God's Son will know beyond the shadow of a doubt that you have eternal life, the reality and not the illusion. And how bold and free we then become in his presence, freely asking according to his will. (vv. 13–15, MSG)

I haven't worked through the whole of this letter counting the number of times we find the word 'know' – a theme throughout the epistle – but in these few verses alone, we find that word seven times in the NIV translation! Sometimes it is knowing about matters of faith; other times it refers to the 'knowing' of relationship. They emphasise the confidence John wants us to have in the basics of our faith and as children of God. So, what does John wants us to be sure about?

He wants us to be sure of eternal life. We are sometimes accused of arrogance when we express certainty about our eternal destiny. It would be arrogance if we based our confidence on ourselves; but it is based entirely on God's free gift to us, through Jesus' death on the cross. Not what we have done, but what he has done.

He wants us to be sure that God hears our prayer. Verse 15 might appear to say that we get whatever we request. But John had heard Jesus say that we must ask 'in Jesus' name' (John 16:23). That is not a perfunctory phrase to add to our prayer; rather it is asking according to his character, with our requests lined up with what he knows is best for us. Those prayers include praying for other Christians who need to change their ways.

He wants us to be sure of our relationship with the Father, sure that he protects his children, despite the evil one's power in this world, and sure of the truths about God and his Son Jesus.

How does this leave us? We can walk joyfully, with our heads held high (but not noses in the air!), humbly knowing that our faith rests on God's love, on the truth of Jesus as the incarnate Son of God who died for us; knowing that we will make mistakes, but that he will keep us from chronic failure.

Thank you, God, that I can be sure of your love as my heavenly Father and for the truth of Jesus as the Son of God. Please help me to live as you want me to, day by day. Amen.

ROSEMARY GREEN

Walk in obedience

Many deceivers, who do not acknowledge Jesus Christ as coming in the flesh, have gone out into the world. Any such person is the deceiver and the antichrist. Watch out that you do not lose what we have worked for, but that you may be rewarded fully. (vv. 7–8, NIV)

Whereas 1 John was a general letter, circulated among many churches around Ephesus, 2 John, also written by John, went to one particular church he knew. 'The lady chosen by God' was not an individual but a congregation; 'her children', its members. John wrote to warn them very specifically, both about the false teaching that was circulating and about the teachers themselves. They were travelling round, sponging on the welcome from Christians. The public inns were usually unsavoury places to stay, so the Christians, expected to show love as Jesus had commanded, were offering their generous hospitality.

Hence this double warning against the teaching and against the teachers. 'It has given me great joy to find some of your children walking in the truth' (v. 4) implies that some of the church members had fallen for the deception. John expected practical love, which included hospitality, but he was strongly against associating with these heretics. 'Anyone who welcomes them shares in their wicked work' (v. 11).

If we are going to apply this to our own lives 2,000 years later, it means that we must learn well God's truths as we find them in the Bible, so that we can be discerning, able to recognise when we are being fed lies. We live in a culture that largely leaves God out of the reckoning or holds strange ideas about him. We may not recognise how easily influenced we are by the unbiblical thinking and attitudes around us. There is a fine line between knowing when we should befriend and seek to influence those who are teaching falsely, or when we should dissociate ourselves from them.

Lord, help me to be diligent to learn and understand your truth, so that I may recognise the lies. Give me your wisdom to know how to reply and to act towards those who are spreading distortions of the truth. Amen.

ROSEMARY GREEN

Hospitality

Diotrephes, who loves to be first, will not welcome us. So when I come, I will call attention to what he is doing, spreading malicious nonsense about us. Not satisfied with that, he even refuses to welcome other believers… Dear friend, do not imitate what is evil but what is good. (vv. 9–11, NIV)

This final letter is written to John's good friend Gaius (one of several men called Gaius in the New Testament), who may have become a Christian through John. 'My children' (v. 4) speaks of three men: Gaius (vv. 1–8), Diotrephes (vv. 9–11a) and Demetrius (v. 12). Gaius was a steadfast Christian, a man of love and truth; John was glad to commend him, particularly for his steadfast faith, his love and his hospitality to visiting Christians, some of them strangers (v. 5).

Diotrephes was diametrically different. He was too keen on his own importance; he loved his position of power, resented John's advice and spread 'malicious nonsense' about him. He turned away visitors himself and discouraged others from welcoming the travelling orthodox preachers. I'm glad I cannot identify a Diotrephes in my church! Demetrius, however, was universally liked and respected, a man who stood up for truth.

We are all called to be hospitable in some way; it is a mark of God's love. Peter expresses it as: 'Offer hospitality to one another without grumbling' (1 Peter 4:9). Another epistle-writer wrote, 'Do not forget to show hospitality to strangers, for by so doing some people have shown hospitality to angels without knowing it' (Hebrews 13:2). We each have different temperaments or gifting and will be hospitable in different ways. I love having people for meals or a simple cuppa but find overnight guests much harder. Some people seem to have a particular gift of hospitality, and warmly welcome any guests, any time. Hospitality is a mark of our generous, welcoming God, and when we extend hospitality, even to strangers, we make him visible (v. 5). It does not have to be in a grand or lavish setting, but it should leave our guests feeling loved and wanting to come again!

Lord, I offer you my home. Please show me how you want me to use it to show your love to others. Amen.

ROSEMARY GREEN

How to pray for our leaders

Catherine Larner writes:

The more uncertain the world is, the more we need good leaders to guide us, reassure us and give us hope and direction in our home, our workplace, our church and our country. Are our current leaders delivering? Are the right people in positions of power and authority?

Certainly, on the world stage we've seen big personalities with big promises. It seems that as we face huge challenges and crises, voters are attracted to the quick, simple solutions being offered by charismatic individuals who draw us in, entertain us, flatter us and help us to feel confident and optimistic.

When these qualities are modelled by our countries' politicians, we often see the same attributes in other people with power and authority in our communities, churches and workplaces. I know I can recall people who have held us spellbound by powerful sermons or speeches, who can turn heads in a crowded room or who know just the right thing to say to change the atmosphere of a meeting or debate. When the laughter, applause or acclamations have died down, what do we see then?

Other than Christ, no one person can provide all we are looking for and, particularly in recent times, we've had examples of charismatic individuals who have displayed evidence of not only poor decision-making but also loose morals, deceit and corruption.

The Bible says that character is what we should be looking for in our leaders, not charisma. 'People look at the outward appearance, but the Lord looks at the heart' (1 Samuel 16:7, NIV).

As the Bible tells us to pray for all those in authority, what do we do when leaders seem to lack integrity and wisdom? We can all pray passionately and with dedication for people we like, but how do we pray for people we don't agree with? How do we respond when it seems the wrong people flourish while others struggle and flounder? How do we pray for bad leaders? What do we do with the resentment, the sense of injustice, the fear and frustration that is in our heart because of this bad leadership? What is God doing in us? How should we be acting?

I hope we shall find answers to some of these questions as we study what the Bible teaches us about praying for our leaders.

The good leader

And what does the Lord require of you? To act justly and to love mercy and to walk humbly with your God. (v. 8, NIV)

We tend to think of leaders as exceptional people with skills, qualities and standards above the norm, who inspire others to achieve their best.

We like leaders to be people of integrity and courage with steadfast, clear and determined beliefs, working for the common good. We like them to have an attractive, appealing personality. With such high expectations placed on them, is it any wonder they often fail?

Working in the media, I am often frustrated at how leaders are forced to adopt polarities, taking one side in a complex issue when sensitive, nuanced discussion is required and how as a society we like to put people on a pedestal only then to find fault, digging into their past for misdemeanours, ridiculing every slip and picking apart any policy or goal. Sometimes we overlook the beliefs or behaviours of people in power entirely and focus instead on their personality because it makes us feel good about ourselves.

We are all called to be leaders after all, whether at home, school, church or work. According to sociologists, even the shyest introvert will influence 10,000 people in their lifetime, and American management guru and pastor John C. Maxwell says leadership is all about influence.

When you are also seeking to uphold Christian principles, there are even more challenges. King Solomon prayed that he would rule with justice, compassion and mercy, bringing harmony and peace (Psalm 72).

Despite having written urging Christians into politics, Tim Farron stood down as leader of the Liberal Democrats in 2017 because he felt 'torn between living as a faithful Christian and serving as a political leader'.

When society is so unforgiving of the failings of its leaders and does not allow people in authority to hold strongly held beliefs or faith, surely only certain individuals will be resilient enough for the role. We need to think about how we respond to bad leaders.

Lord, I pray that you will protect our leaders, keeping them humble, gracious and full of integrity. Give them the courage and wisdom to do what's right, not what's popular. Amen.

CATHERINE LARNER

We get the leaders we deserve

I urge, then, first of all, that petitions, prayers, intercession and thanksgiving be made for all people – for kings and all those in authority, that we may live peaceful and quiet lives in all godliness and holiness. (vv. 1–2, NIV)

There isn't a great deal of respect for leaders today. We see people in positions of authority differently from previous generations. Doctors no longer wear white coats and they want to be known by their first names, business owners like to mix with their employees, parents want to be friends with their children and politicians often forgo the use of a hairbrush or wearing a tie and appear on popular television shows.

In some ways this lack of deference for status and position might be commended. If we look to our leadership model in Christ, the good shepherd, he was called to live among his sheep and was concerned with building strong relationships over time. However, the pressure of today's society seems to be a quick fix with often superficial connections.

A French philosopher in the 18th century coined the phrase 'we get the leaders we deserve' and certainly in a democracy the majority has voted for a government. But in churches, often elders appoint a minister and a management team will select a director. We aren't always involved in the decision-making, or perhaps we favoured the other candidate. What do we do when not only is someone not suitable for the role, but they also seem incompetent or dangerous?

God wants us to respect our rulers. In Romans 13:1, we read that they have been appointed by him. So, whether they are godly or corrupt, we need to lift them to the Lord, asking for his intervention – giving them the qualities of servant leadership and working through them, or in spite of them, to further his purposes. We don't see the complete picture so, for the moment, we need to do our part by faithfully praying.

Lord, shine your light in our homes, churches, businesses and governments to bring truth and justice. May your Spirit convict those in power of wrongdoing, that they may turn away from sin and seek your will in their lives. Amen.

CATHERINE LARNER

Cry out to God

'I looked for someone among them who would build up the wall and stand before me in the gap on behalf of the land so I would not have to destroy it, but I found no one.' (v. 30, NIV)

Sometimes we see terrible things done by those in positions of trust and power. It can lead us to cry out in anguish, frustration and despair. What does our Lord expect of us when we learn of inexcusable acts? How do we deal with our disappointment in leaders?

When Samuel's mother entrusted her son into the care of the high priest, Eli, she thought she was doing the very best for him. But Eli was a weak man who allowed his sons to abuse their privileges as priests. Seeing his mentor failing him, Samuel could have floundered, but he kept his eyes on God and became one of Israel's greatest prophets. The Jews were released from captivity when God worked through the life of the pagan King Cyrus of Persia; the Roman leaders facilitated the crucifixion of Christ (Acts 2:23) – God's purposes can be fulfilled through, and in spite of, bad leaders.

In more recent times, John F. Kennedy was unfaithful to his wife, but God used his courage to stand against communist Russia in Cuba. The Conservative MP Jonathan Aitken was imprisoned for perjury but became an Anglican priest and is honorary president of Christian Solidarity Worldwide.

There are examples throughout the Old Testament of people of God who interceded for corrupt nations and leaders. Abraham prayed for Sodom (Genesis 18:22–25) and Joshua pleaded the people's case before God when Achan sinned (Joshua 7:6–9).

We can lift up our nations and pray that God will work among us, that good will overcome evil and that our leaders may work for the greater good despite their personal failures and sins.

When sometimes we can be overcome by terrible people and events, isn't it exciting and liberating to think God might be working through situations where we cannot possibly see the positive outcomes?

Lord, show me how to pray. Hear my plea for my nation, my workplace, my church, my home. Do something new! Work through bad leaders to do good. Amen.

CATHERINE LARNER

It's too easy to criticise

Do not let any unwholesome talk come out of your mouths, but only what is helpful for building others up according to their needs, that it may benefit those who listen. (v. 29, NIV)

Jesus called out corruption and injustice throughout his ministry and there are times when we should speak out against bad practices. But we need to do so wisely and respectfully. It's too easy to criticise, isn't it? So often I find that I can see ways in which things may be done differently or (seemingly) more successfully, but actually putting processes in place, getting systems running, achieving goals and keeping people happy is not easy. So, when is it right to challenge a leader? Are we exhibiting arrogance in assuming that we know best?

I remember a work situation where a colleague was appointed to a higher role. They weren't equipped or experienced for the position and the fact that they were dependent on the team to not only support them but cover their failings, while also receiving a higher salary, all seemed unjust. What's more, their inadequacy seemed to be hindering the progress of the organisation as a whole.

But there was a choice in our responses – we could focus on all the problems and weaknesses and let our bitterness fester, or we could prayerfully raise the situation with our superiors, then forgive the individual, offer them love and acceptance and hand the situation over to God.

People will always let us down, but God will never fail us. Instead of spending time and energy finding fault, we should be wise and sensitive to people who are struggling and fix our eyes on Christ and follow his example.

After acknowledging the difficulties of a situation and handing it to the Lord, it can be liberating to focus on our relationship with him, standing firm in our faith.

Lord, I'm struggling to respond to this situation in a way which is honouring to you. This leader seems to be thwarting your purposes, but help me to respond in a way which is pleasing to you. Amen.

CATHERINE LARNER

Bring about change

'Is not this the kind of fasting I have chosen: to loose the chains of injustice and untie the cords of the yoke… to share your food with the hungry and to provide the poor wanderer with shelter?' (vv. 6–7, NIV)

Bad leaders might not always be bad people. In fact, they're usually just like us – men and women trying to do their best but who make mistakes. If we put our leaders on a pedestal, they are likely to let us down. We can't expect them to be right about everything. Certainly, any leadership or management role today is hugely demanding.

We don't have to be passive and accept injustice, but we should model Christlike behaviour when entering into a dispute. Jesus said: 'Love your neighbour as yourself' (Matthew 22:39), and that meant people we don't get on with as well as those we do!

We shouldn't rely solely on leaders being the answer. I recently met a doctor whose first posting was to serve in a hospital just as the pandemic hit. Though she has spoken extensively about her experience, the failings of the system and how she would like to see things improved by decision-makers, she didn't feel this was sufficient. 'It wasn't enough to sit huddled in a corner complaining,' she said. 'I wanted to help bring about change.' And she became a local councillor.

It's easy to pick fault, to join with the naysayers and grumble about poor decisions made by a superior, but it's much more difficult to take responsibility or to offer a better alternative.

In Isaiah 58, the people are praying and fasting against the injustice in the land, and God hears them, but he also requires them to act, to be the answer to their prayers.

We can complain, vote and protest, but we can also show kindness and contribute. We can help to be the solution. We can pray for bad leaders while also doing something about the situation ourselves!

Lord, thank you for the thousands of local authority workers and councillors who serve their communities with such dedication, care and compassion. Give me courage to help those seeking to overcome evil with good. Amen.

CATHERINE LARNER

Trusting in God

'Don't let your hearts be troubled. Trust in God, and trust also in me.'
(v. 1, NLT)

There is a danger in putting too much store on an individual. Whether a good leader or not, we shouldn't be consumed by evaluating their performance. We cannot absolve responsibility for our decisions, standards and behaviours. We have seen this in the church as well as in wider society. A charismatic, passionate and effective leader can do no wrong, until there is a massive fall from grace and the followers are lost and broken.

Instead of putting all our confidence in an individual, we should be looking at the bigger picture – the greater good – working together as a community, following Jesus and trusting that God has everything in hand.

I often recall the image of life being like a tapestry. On the finished side every stitch is perfectly in place, a colourful, intricate and beautiful design. On the back, all the workings are evident. Particularly with the way I sew, the tapestry is a mess of knots and loose threads, and the pattern is a shadow of the final picture.

Corrie ten Boom often quoted a poem which used this same analogy called 'The Master Weaver's Plan': 'For he can view the pattern upon the upper side, while I can see it only on this, the underside.'

Life may be tough, and we can struggle to understand how and why some people are in power, but God is above it all; trusting that he has everything in hand is reassuring and exciting. We don't have the whole picture at the moment, but we trust in our good and faithful God. We can look to do our part no matter how seemingly insignificant it may feel. We put our trust in God, not in our leaders.

Lord, please work through our nation. I will pray for our leaders, but I will keep my faith in you, for I place my hope in you. Amen.

CATHERINE LARNER

Seeking God's will

'You are the light of the world… let your good deeds shine out for all to see, so that everyone will praise your heavenly Father.' (v. 14 and v. 16, NLT)

When people hold positions of power and responsibility, we want to see them do good things. When they are not as capable as I expect or are more concerned with their own interests rather than the greater good, I am disappointed, frustrated and disillusioned.

Instead of being dragged down by a bad situation, though, I'm trying to find ways to respond that seek God's will and help me grow in faith and character. It's still very much a work in progress!

While we pray for and support our godly leaders, asking for them to be wise, to be courageous and to follow Christ's model, we should also pray for God to work his purposes out through the ungodly leaders. We ask that they might turn away from evil practices and seek good.

We might get alongside the leader, like Jonathan and David, and be a listening ear, a guide, a mentor even. 'Without wise leadership, a nation falls; there is safety in having many advisers' (Proverbs 11:14).

If we need to challenge the leader, we should do so with kindness, remembering always that we are called to be peacemakers, seeking love and unity in all situations. We should stand firm in our faith and show grace to those who do not yet believe.

The central abiding principle for Christians is to remember Christ's commandment to love one another. Love and unity are central to the Christian message and the Christian witness. Instead of complaining about evil, we can look at how we can do good ourselves.

Lord, I pray that your will be done through both godly and ungodly leaders, and that you will lead me to act and speak wisely, bringing your light to shine in the darkness. Amen.

CATHERINE LARNER

Singleness, through the lens of the Bible

Ruth Akinradewo writes:

What do I know about being single? At 27, I realise there are many others who have much more extensive experience of living as a single person, but I believe I have learned a lot not only through my own experience, but also through studying God's word and learning from those around me; whether they are married, single, in a relationship or fit into other brackets.

It's hard to avoid talk of relationship status these days. Society accords a great deal of value to who we romantically love, when we love them and why. Perhaps that's because 'significant others' have a big part to play in our lives. Usually, we live with them. We might have children with them. Our choice of romantic partner often says a lot about who we are: their interests are often intermingled with ours, their hopes and desires shaped and shared by us too. If so much collective value is accorded to a romantic partner, what happens when we don't have one?

There's no question that the Bible teaches us plenty about how to live in the sanctity of marriage, but it also has much to teach us about how to live well as a single person. In my experience, we tend to talk a lot less about this. But as we probably spend the most time with ourselves, shouldn't we learn to spend that time well?

Furthermore, I believe the Bible challenges our thinking about single-hood and single people. For example, many conversations about single-hood in the global church revolve around the axis of marriage, where being single is often regarded as an interim season before the 'better thing' comes along. Is this a picture drawn by the Bible?

It's interesting that Paul, the man who laid out so much guidance for married couples in the scriptures, was, in fact, single. Isn't it noteworthy that the man who Christians follow, Jesus Christ, was, in fact, unmarried? Do we stop to consider that the first human witness to Jesus' resurrection was, in fact, a single woman?

I'm excited to delve further into what the Bible teaches us about the gift of singleness. I pray that God will reveal new things to us as we study this fascinating theme together through the lens of his word and the characters in his story.

Created for relationship

And the Lord God said, '*It is* not good that man should be alone; I will make him a helper comparable to him.' (v. 18, NKJV)

I was 19 years old when people in my social circle started to make the first remarks (partly in jest, partly seriously!) about how it would be my turn next to walk down the aisle. (I didn't agree!) The line we most often hear when it comes to the expectation of marriage is: 'It is not good that man should be alone.' But what does this really mean?

In Genesis 1, God sets out the standard for how we are to live. Created in the image of the trinitarian maker, we are designed to reflect him. The words, 'Let Us make man in Our image, according to Our likeness' (1:26), indicate clearly that God is, in very nature, an interpersonal God. Here is the perfectly unmatched image of unity in diversity: one God in three persons.

Humankind's very existence is centred upon interconnectedness. Adam's first assignment is to tend to the plants in the garden of Eden. It is shortly after this that God first remarks: 'It is not good that man should be alone.' He subsequently forms the animals and entrusts them to Adam's care. Though now surrounded by multiple creatures, God reveals that none of them are either comparable to Adam or able to help him fulfil his purpose. What does this tell us? Our relationship to the earth and to animals does not suffice if we are to live in the fullness of life that the Creator has ordained for his children.

God does not desire for us to go about our lives in isolation. We are created for relationship: primarily, relationship with God, and then relationship with one another.

Regardless of marital status, we are each called by God to 'do life' with others. Are we doing so?

Do you struggle with isolation? Whether married or single, God desires you to live your life in community with others. Ask God to lead you to the right relationships with those around you, that his will may be accomplished.

RUTH AKINRADEWO

The eternal husband

For your Maker *is* your husband, The Lord of hosts *is* His name; And your Redeemer *is* the Holy One of Israel; He is called the God of the whole earth. (v. 5, NKJV)

We often refer to Jesus' followers worldwide as 'the body of Christ'. At times, we may substitute this for 'the bride of Christ'. In the apostle Paul's famous teachings on marriage (for example, Ephesians 5:23–32), he likens the union between a husband and wife to the self-sacrificing love demonstrated by Jesus to us, his body.

Today's passage in Isaiah makes it known loud and clear: our creator, the almighty God, has redeemed us and given us his name. In biblical times, women had very little status in society and were defined by their relationship to their husbands; thus, a woman rejected by her husband became a social pariah, clothed in shame. In this love letter to Israel, God describes his people as being like a heartbroken woman abandoned by her spouse. Yet in his love, God has called her by name and covered her with his glory.

This is our God. There is 'no partiality with God' (Romans 2:11). Whether married, divorced, single or widowed, he covers us *all* with his glory and gives us *all* his name. Society and Christian culture may fall into the habit of ranking us according to our relationship status, but God accords no eternal significance to our marital state – he cares for the states of our hearts and the salvation of our souls.

What is more, Jesus tells us that there will be no marrying in heaven: 'For in the resurrection they neither marry nor are given in marriage, but are like angels of God in heaven' (Matthew 22:30). So it is futile for us to focus on marriage between man and woman as the greatest manifestation of holiness: indeed, the epitome of holiness is to worship our eternal husband with all that we are, for all our days on earth and then beyond.

What is your response, considering God as both your maker and your husband? Have you ever felt shame regarding your marital status or, indeed, pride? Ask God to reveal to you what it means to be his bride.

RUTH AKINRADEWO

Marriage isn't for everyone

Jesus replied, 'Not everyone can accept this word, but only those to whom it has been given... there are those who choose to live like eunuchs for the sake of the kingdom of heaven. The one who can accept this should accept it.' (vv. 11–12, NIV)

For some of us, marriage is a deep desire. For others, it might never have been, and suddenly you find that God has changed your mind by bringing you a godly spouse! Still others may feel certain that the best thing for them is to stay single.

Delighting ourselves in the Lord (Psalm 37:4) does not necessarily yield the results we desire, even when what we desire is good. In 2 Corinthians 12, the apostle Paul describes asking God to remove his 'thorn in my flesh' (v. 7), which we understand to be some form of physical ailment. God's response? 'My grace is sufficient for you, for my power is made perfect in weakness' (v. 9).

We are called to believe in faith that God will answer our prayers; however, we are simultaneously urged to trust that his actions towards us are always motivated by love. Our lives are designed to reflect his desires for us – we fit into his plan. Our Father's way is not our way (Isaiah 55:8), painful though that reality might sometimes be!

We are not all meant to be married. In this passage, Jesus acknowledges that not everybody is graced with the ability to live the long-term single life. He also recognises that those who *do* remain single do so for different reasons: some may stay single because they lack sexual desire, others may be celibate as a result of surgical changes and others might personally decide to remain unmarried for the furtherance of God's kingdom on earth.

God's grace is sufficient for whatever we are called to be. If we are to be married, he gives us what we need for that season in time; if we are to remain single, his grace will empower us there, too.

Whatever we choose for ourselves and wherever God directs us, our greatest calling remains to seek God's kingdom here on earth. Ask God for the wisdom to make choices in your personal life that will further his kingdom.

RUTH AKINRADEWO

Single-minded

There is a difference between a wife and a virgin. The unmarried woman cares about the things of the Lord, that she may be holy both in body and in spirit. But she who is married cares about the things of the world – how she may please *her* husband. (v. 34, NKJV)

It may seem ironic that you're reading about the pros of singlehood on Valentine's Day! 'I wish everyone were single, just as I am. Yet each person has a special gift from God, of one kind or another,' Paul writes in his letter to the Corinthians (NLT).

The most prolific writer of the New Testament, Paul went from persecuting Christians to devotedly serving Christ and his bride, after encountering the splendour of the Lord Jesus for himself. Paul knows what it is like to try life apart from God. He later comes to recognise that nothing can separate us from the everlasting love of God (Romans 8:38–39). Post-conversion, Paul is committed to pursuing deeper intimacy with the one he calls 'Lord'.

Paul considers singleness a gift; it enables him to focus single-mindedly on his relationship with his creator. He does not condemn those who wish to marry or, indeed, those already espoused, but rather desires the church to know that an unmarried person, unburdened by romantic attachments, has fewer distractions on their path.

Verses 36–38 make clear that singleness may not be a lifelong calling; it may be beneficial for a time. None of us are born married and for most of us it's not on the cards until at least our 20s, therefore, most of us can, for a season, focus unadulteratedly on developing greater intimacy with God – without spousal responsibilities added.

Are you single? How are you spending this season? Undoubtedly there are things that you can accomplish for the kingdom of God in this time of singleness that you wouldn't be able to do in the same way later, should you get married. Are you married? How do you think of your single friends? Do you focus on getting them matched off or do you encourage them to flourish in kingdom-building right where they are?

Lord, thank you that you are the giver of all good gifts. Thank you for gracing me with what I need for this season. May I seek first your kingdom in all things, encouraging others to do the same. Amen.

RUTH AKINRADEWO

Jesus: the ultimate example

**'You know what has happened throughout the province of Judea…
how God anointed Jesus of Nazareth with the Holy Spirit and power,
and how he went around doing good and healing all who were under
the power of the devil, because God was with him.' (vv. 37–38, NIV)**

How does one sum up the stellar example that Jesus provides for us all?
Here is a single person optimising their life for the service of the kingdom.
Jesus' focus was unmatched: he was to save his people from their sins
and reveal God the Father to them. This he did, without a wife by his side!

Jesus never married, but he did fulfil his vocation in relationship
with others. His many disciples were essential to the spreading of the
good news.

Is it relevant that Jesus was single? I think so. Just think of the number
of times Christ was on his way somewhere and was stopped by someone
wanting a miracle! I reckon most wives wouldn't be too happy about
their husbands regularly returning home much later than planned! Also,
how happy would you be if thousands of women talked about loving
your husband?

As we explored yesterday, being unmarried meant that Jesus could
go about his God-given mission without the responsibilities – and even
distractions – that could come with having a wife.

As I reflect on my own life, I recognise that being single has given me
the freedom to serve God in different ways. For example, touring with a
Christian drama ministry through several different countries, committing
to leading church activities and giving my time to charitable causes.

None of us wants to look back on our lives wishing that we had done
more for God. No matter where you are in life, it's not too late to make a
change. You have a ministry right where you are: God is with you, and he
has anointed you with power. Now, go about doing good.

---

*Are you single, realising that you haven't fully appreciated the freedom you
have to be used by God now? Are you married? How can you go about doing
good for God where you are? There is plenty to do!*

RUTH AKINRADEWO

Mary

Then they said to her, 'Woman, why are you weeping?' She said to them, 'Because they have taken away my Lord, and I do not know where they have laid Him'... Jesus said to her, 'Mary!' She turned and said to Him, 'Rabboni!' (John 20:13, 16, NKJV)

Yesterday we considered the person of Jesus. Today, we're looking at the person who first saw him living and breathing following his crucifixion three days before. Her name was Mary Magdalene, and she was a single woman.

We know little about her; the only clear details given in the scriptures about Mary Magdalene's life away from Jesus are that she was possessed by seven demons until Jesus sent them packing.

Mary is indebted to Jesus for her freedom. The Bible describes her as following Jesus and taking care of his needs before his crucifixion. Mary Magdalene is also one of the women who witnesses her Saviour being cruelly killed. She is there when he is buried.

For the stupendous revelation of his greatest miracle, Jesus chooses Mary to be the very first person to see him. He calls her by name, in a voice rich with love, and she knows then that her Saviour has done what he promised all along: he has risen from the dead on the third day – and there he stands, before her.

How amazing is it that Jesus chooses a single woman to be the first eyewitness to the most miraculous event in history? It is no secret that God loves to use those whom the world would never choose, for his glory (1 Corinthians 1:20–21).

Women's voices were little considered in the days of Jesus, still less the voices of single women. Yet the Son of God chose a single woman to tell the most remarkable news in history. What does that say to us?

The very existence of a church known as a 'single-friendly church' indicates that many churches overlook single people when it comes to ministry. How can we change this?

RUTH AKINRADEWO

The Samaritan woman

The woman answered and said, 'I have no husband'. Jesus said to her, 'You have well said, "I have no husband," for you have had five husbands, and the one whom you now have is not your husband; in that you spoke truly.' (vv. 17–18, NKJV)

The woman we meet today has often been portrayed as a loose woman – someone who liked shopping for husbands – but the real story is rather different. Women in biblical times had virtually no legal rights, and thus, the Samaritan woman was never the one to instigate a divorce – it was always the man who held the keys.

What is more, the Samaritan woman may never have been divorced. By the customs of the day, if a woman's husband passed away without having children, his brother or the next male relative was to marry his widow. It could well be that the Samaritan woman's five husbands had all died.

Another explanation sometimes considered today is that the Samaritan woman struggled with infertility. A man's ability to bear children meant that he could continue his name and pass his wealth down; as such, pro-creation was regarded as a vital part of maintaining status. In the fiercely patriarchal society of the time, if the Samaritan woman was unable to bear children, she would have been ripe for rejection.

When she meets Jesus, the man with whom she lives has not even married her: thus, she has no real legal protection. She is a social outcast and forced to draw water at the hottest part of the day.

Imagine her surprise, therefore, when Jesus speaks to her! Not only is he a man, but he is a Jew! And Jews 'have no dealings with Samaritans' (v. 9). I can picture her double take. I can see her looking back, thinking: *Is there someone behind me?* Surely, he is not addressing her.

But he is! And he is offering her living water.

Can you relate to the rejection this woman experienced or do you know others who can? Take the time to pray for them (or yourself) now.

RUTH AKINRADEWO

Anna

Anna, a prophetess… was of a great age, and had lived with a husband seven years from her virginity; and this woman *was* a widow of about eighty-four years, who did not depart from the temple, but served God with fastings and prayers night and day. (vv. 36–37, NKJV)

It isn't clear whether Anna had been a widow for 84 years, or was a woman aged 84. What is clear is that she has known life as a widow for longer than she was single pre-marriage, and she has been widowed for much longer than she was married.

Anna, the widowed prophetess, is one of the first to behold the new-born Immanuel. Imagine the delight that must have illuminated her face upon seeing the promised Saviour, he whom she had spent years assuring her fellow worshippers would come.

Anna's devotion to the Lord is evident: she spends countless hours praying and fasting in the temple before she witnesses the fulfilment of age-old prophecies in Christ. She is honoured with the privilege of seeing the glory of the Lord in the flesh.

Decades of following the Lord will have rendered Anna a bastion of wisdom; I imagine that when she spoke ceaselessly of Jesus to those in search of the redeemer, people listened.

Titus 2:3–7 speaks about how older women should teach those who are younger how to be good wives and mothers, but its exhortation is much broader. As we have already explored, our first and eternal husband as Christ-followers is the Lord Jesus. There is much we can learn from those who love him well. Anna is a prime example of an older woman showing the younger how it's done!

I have wonderful women in my life who I consider spiritual mothers. Some are married; some are not. What I continue to learn from them is priceless: they are wisdom-filled examples of how to better love my maker.

Can you think of older women who have inspired you to grow in your faith? Consider how you can be a 'spiritual mother' to those around you, telling them of the glory of God as Anna did in her community.

RUTH AKINRADEWO

Lydia: Europe's first Christian convert

Now a certain woman named Lydia heard *us*. She was a seller of purple from the city of Thyatira, who worshipped God. The Lord opened her heart to heed the things spoken by Paul. (v. 14, NKJV)

I'm going to be honest, when I think of Lydia, I tend to remember her as the woman who sold purple cloth!

I'm sure you can think of several women in the scriptures who were prayer warriors. Anna of yesterday's study was one; Hannah the mother of Samuel was another; and Lydia of today's passage is among them! There's a lot more to her than first meets the eye.

God directs the apostle Paul to Philippi, and it is during this trip that he meets Lydia. The words 'seller of purple' reveal a lot about her. Lydia is an established businesswoman in her community – purple cloth was an in-demand, expensive luxury item. To stay in business, she must have acquired a number of affluent customers. What is more, Lydia originates from Thyatira (in modern-day Turkey), a city at the cutting edge of trade. She is a woman of considerable influence.

Not many women at this time were described as women of influence without also being described as somebody's wife. There is no mention of a husband here; yet Lydia is the embodiment of the Proverbs 31 woman: she is industrious, God-fearing and cares for her household. She is also the first-documented convert to Christianity in Europe.

Forbidden from worshipping God within Philippi's gates, Lydia gathers with other women to pray regularly. Though not born into the Jewish tradition, she has chosen to follow God. She seals the deal by getting baptised.

And finally, she shows hospitality not just in heart, but in deeds, by inviting Paul and the other missionaries to stay at the home she shares with others.

Lydia is a woman of determination, diligence, prayer and hospitality. I want to be like her!

Read Proverbs 31:10–31. Have you tended to associate this solely with a 'virtuous wife'? How much would your holistic approach to Christian living change if you considered this standard to apply to you, whether married or not?

RUTH AKINRADEWO

Tabitha

At Joppa there was a certain disciple named Tabitha, which is translated Dorcas. This woman was full of good works and charitable deeds which she did. (v. 36, NKJV)

When you die, wouldn't you like to be described as a woman 'full of good works and charitable deeds'? I would!

When Tabitha, or Dorcas, dies from an illness, that is how she is remembered. A host of widows gather to mourn by her bedside, distraught at the loss of a woman whose presence has meant so much to their community. They send for Jesus' disciple Peter to come, desperate for a miracle that will see Dorcas restored to them.

It is striking that as Peter arrives, the widows clutch at and show him the garments that Tabitha made for them in her lifetime: they represent the physical remnants of the love that she so freely gave to the people of Joppa.

Before she dies, Tabitha is an example of Christlike kindness and empathy. The light and fragrance which emanate from her are so tangible that her community immediately feels the enormity of her loss.

And then, in her *second* life, Tabitha draws attention to the supernatural wonder of God! She is, in fact, the first person to be raised from the dead by any of the disciples, after Jesus himself arises from the grave. What a testimony!

It is likely that Tabitha was a widow, especially as many of those who surround her deathbed are widows. Yet she is known for her generosity of spirit. Her status is defined not by her marital status, but by how she chooses to spend her time. She devotes her life to the service of others and is rewarded by God with life on earth afresh, and her place in God's book.

I often think about how I would like to be remembered when I die. Do you? How would you want to be described in the account of your life?

Do you consider kindness and charitable work a ministry? How can you be part of making a positive impact on those in need in your community?

RUTH AKINRADEWO

Shamelessly expensive gratitude

A woman in the city who was a sinner… brought an alabaster flask of fragrant oil, and stood at [Jesus'] feet behind *Him* weeping; and she began to wash His feet with her tears, and wiped *them* with the hair of her head; and she kissed His feet. (vv. 37–38, NKJV)

'I will be *even more* undignified than this' (2 Samuel 6:22, my emphasis), King David shamelessly answers as he is mocked for putting aside all decorum and worshipping God with unbridled joy; this sticks in my mind as I read this passage. Imagine this: you're in the company of the holiest man in town, and a woman turns up uninvited, makes a beeline for said holy man, lavishes expensive oil on him and then begins to wash and kiss his feet! How would you react if you were hosting that party?

Simon the Pharisee isn't impressed. He doesn't say a word, but perhaps a flicker – or more – of condescension traverses his face. In any case, Jesus knows exactly what Simon is thinking. This woman's reputation – she is most likely a prostitute – has gone before her.

If I were at a party and anyone walked in and started kissing another guest's feet in front of me, I would feel uncomfortable. To be quite frank, I feel uncomfortable even reading this account. What an intimate expression of love!

Perhaps it is precisely because this account makes some of us uncomfortable that it is featured in the scriptures. Most of us like to worship God in a way that is deemed acceptable. We don't want to be too 'out there'.

This woman doesn't care. She knows the magnitude of her sins, but she knows, too, of the greatness of Jesus' love. She knows she is making a scene, but she believes the Messiah to be worthy of her most undignified worship. For worship isn't about how she looks; it's about how he looks.

Yet, when this woman leaves, she looks much better than when she entered: her face may be tear-stained, but her slate has been wiped clean.

Have you ever struggled with sexual sin – when single, during marraige or even after marriage? God's love covers a multitude of sins. He does not condemn you, but lovingly calls you to 'sin no more'. Lay it all down at his feet.

RUTH AKINRADEWO

Martha: a sister of great faith

Now Martha said to Jesus, 'Lord, if You had been here, my brother would not have died. But even now I know that whatever You ask of God, God will give You.' (John 11:21, NKJV)

Martha, Lazarus' sister, deserves more credit than we typically give her. Often singled out as the sister not to emulate because she is more focused on hosting duties than on sitting at Jesus' feet, it's easy to skim over her part in the Jesus story. We won't do that today.

Martha clearly enjoys serving other people. She does at times get carried away, taken more by 'doing' than 'being', but there are enough references made to her welcoming, serving and preparing meals for guests that we can safely assume she has the gift of hospitality. Like Lydia, she has a knack for building community by taking care of people's needs. Maybe Martha just gives too much headspace to how long the bread has been in the oven and whether there are enough goblets for everyone! Her brain and her body will certainly fare much better when she stills herself to enjoy the presence of God.

The counterpoint to Martha's over-investment in transient things is the incredible faith she displays when Jesus returns to Bethany after the death of her brother, Lazarus. She demonstrates an out-of-this-world perspective: though Lazarus has been dead for four days, she knows instinctively that Jesus, her friend and the Son of God, has the power to change the story.

This does not mean she does not doubt. I mean, who wouldn't, having witnessed the death of a loved one four days prior? It's completely reasonable that Martha was less than keen on having the odour of her brother's corpse released into the environs.

However, her earlier words testify of her faith. 'Yes, Lord, I believe that You are the Christ, the Son of God, who is to come into the world' (v. 27). Jesus honours her faith. He brings her brother back to life.

Do you often slip into 'doing' rather than 'being'? So do I! Remember, though, the faith that you hold: no matter the situation, God can turn it around – and sometimes you don't need to do anything other than have faith.

RUTH AKINRADEWO

Ruth

'It has been fully reported to me, all that you have done for your mother-in-law since the death of your husband, and *how* you have left your father and your mother and the land of your birth, and have come to a people whom you did not know before.' (v. 11, NKJV)

There is a widely held belief that two biologically unrelated women cannot dwell together in harmony. Whether a man's wife and his mother, or two women sharing the figurative stage of success, we are often painted as naturally predisposed to compete against, rather than cheer for one another.

Well, doesn't the story of Ruth and Naomi turn that stereotype on its head?

Naomi is a broken woman by the end of chapter 1. Already displaced from her homeland due to famine, she experiences further loss when her husband dies. Ten years pass, and then both her sons die. It's easy to see why Naomi feels bitter about how her life has turned out. When she leaves Bethlehem, she enjoys the protection that comes with having three male family members. When she returns, she is a widow bereft.

We can hardly avoid the preeminence placed on marriage here: Naomi's hopes of her daughters-in-law having a better life are dependent upon them getting married again. Moreover, Naomi's despair about her own future is tied to the thought that she is too old to marry.

Still, Ruth is determined to be Naomi's protection. Orpah journeys resolutely with her mother-in-law for some time, but eventually she gives in to Naomi's pleas and returns to Moab. Ruth does not. She is determined to stay by her mother-in-law's side, to learn the customs of her land and to follow Naomi's God. Ruth's unwavering loyalty is described as *hesed*, a Hebrew term used to depict God's steadfast, covenant love for his people.

Ruth's extraordinary acts of love do not go unnoticed. Boaz praises her self-sacrificial kindness towards Naomi and her service to God and pronounces a blessing over Ruth. (Did he have any hopes for how that might play out, I wonder?)

Even for those who do marry, wedded bliss may not last forever. Ruth spent her time as a young widow taking care of a woman who was both her mother-in-law and her spiritual mother. What a beautiful act of loyal love!

RUTH AKINRADEWO

The widowed single parent

Then the word of the Lord came to [Elijah]: 'Go at once to Zarephath in the region of Sidon and stay there. I have instructed a widow there to supply you with food.' (vv. 8–9, NIV)

Just like that, we became a family of four: a widow and her three children. I was 13 when our dad died.

The scriptures are filled with commands to care for the widows and those without parents. Psalm 68:5 describes God as the 'father to the fatherless, a defender of widows', one who 'sets the lonely in families' (Psalm 68:6).

Today we are looking at the unnamed widow of Zarephath (in modern-day Lebanon), who demonstrates a willingness to be like the Christian widow described in 1 Timothy 5:10. She hosts and feeds the prophet Elijah during a season of drought, despite having a son to care for. As I write this, I cannot help but think of the many single-parent families struggling to make ends meet during an unparalleled cost-of-living crisis.

Growing up in a single-parent family, I can attest to God's faithfulness as my mum held down a successful career, served generously at church and concurrently raised three children in the knowledge and fear of God. My mum is amazing and an inspiration to me.

I am also inspired by a close family friend, who recalls God assuring her that he would be a father to her children when her husband left her and she found herself a single parent. She tells me: 'God has never failed to keep that promise.'

God sent Elijah to Zarephath to reveal that he was Jehovah Jireh – the Lord our Provider. The eternal husband and the loving Father. Elijah arrives when the widow has only a handful of flour and a few drops of oil remaining. Yet somehow, God supplies her and her son's every need (Philippians 4:19) – and Elijah's, too!

How incredible is it that the widow of Zarephath provides for Elijah when her own future looks so bleak? Pray for single parents who feel at their wits' end today. If you are struggling, know that the Lord is your provider too.

RUTH AKINRADEWO

Psalm 37: how to live in an imperfect world

Jackie Harris writes:

I know several people who have stopped listening to or reading the news, at least for a period of time, because they found it too difficult to cope with. So much seems to be going wrong that it is hard not to get anxious or angry about what is happening in the world. We don't have to look far to see injustice, indulgence and unfairness. How do we avoid falling into despair or letting our own standards slip away? Psalm 37 offers some wise advice.

It is attributed to David, writing as an old man (v. 25) and seeking to share his wisdom and experience with a younger generation troubled by what they saw happening around them. While there were many who sought to follow God's ways, there were others who were influenced by the Canaanites, descendants of the original inhabitants of the promised land, known for their wickedness. Things were not as they should be, and David wanted to encourage the faithful to trust God despite the injustices they saw around them.

Psalm 37 is one of the wisdom psalms and reads rather like the book of Proverbs. It is also an acrostic psalm, a strict style where each verse begins with a different letter of the Hebrew alphabet. Perhaps it was written this way to help people remember David's teaching. Certainly there is lots of repetition as David drives home his message that God is faithful, and that wickedness will be dealt with. In the end, all will be well. The wicked will be punished and the righteous rewarded, and those punishments and rewards will be permanent. In the meantime, God's people are to focus on God and to follow his ways.

What David gives us in this psalm is a toolkit to help us live in an imperfect world. These tools include developing the right mindset so that things don't get on top of us, paying attention to what we say and do and reminding ourselves of God's sovereignty, his promises and his provision for us. David's core message is that we can trust God both now and for the future.

As we begin this study, let's bring to mind those things that trouble us, remembering that while we may live in an imperfect world, our God is perfect: 'A faithful God who does no wrong, upright and just is he' (Deuteronomy 32:4, NIV).

Don't fret!

Do not fret because of those who are evil or be envious of those who do wrong; for like the grass they will soon wither, like green plants they will soon die away. (vv. 1–2, NIV)

At a particularly challenging time in my life, I was reminded that we have no control over the things that happen, but we can choose how we react. However, before we can do the right thing, we have to think the right thing. David recognised this, so begins with the instruction: 'Do not fret'.

The word translated as 'fret' is full of meaning. It suggests a mixture of worry and anxiety, anger and resentment. In other words, we are not to get wound up about what we see happening around us. Instead of going over and over the things that irritate us or make us anxious, we should deliberately turn our attention to God and his trustworthiness (v. 3).

This is not always easy to do, but David gives us a step-by-step guide to help us bring our thoughts into line. First, we turn to God in trust – we hand over to him the things that concern us and threaten to overwhelm us, confident that he can handle them (v. 3). Second, we turn our attention to doing good (v. 3). How can we reflect God's goodness to the world and bless those around us? Third, we take time to enjoy the blessings God has already given us (v. 3). Then, we make a conscious decision to seek more of God. Delighting in the Lord (v. 4) involves spending time with him, seeking to know him better and meditating on his goodness and love. In doing so, we redirect our emotions away from fear and worry to praise, thanksgiving and peace.

But there's more. When we delight in God, we are changed. The desires of our hearts become more and more aligned with God's own desires for our lives, and it is his delight to give us more of himself. This is the meaning of the wonderful promise in verse 4.

Do you need to change your thinking today? Bring to God anything that is making you anxious or upset and then spend some time meditating on God's sovereignty and goodness.

JACKIE HARRIS

Submit and be still

Commit your way to the Lord; trust in him... Be still before the Lord and wait patiently for him. (v. 5 and v. 7, NIV)

Yesterday, we were thinking about our thought patterns – what we dwell on – and we ended with the wonderful promise that God gives us more of himself when we delight in him. In these next three verses, David explains more of what it means to delight in God. It involves submission and still-ness, two disciplines that seem countercultural today.

When David talks about committing your way to the Lord, he doesn't mean that we bring our plans to him to get them rubberstamped! It's more about bringing our plans to God to check that they are in line with his plans. But it's deeper than that. It's about trusting God enough to sur-render our ways to his ways. I find this hugely challenging, but it underlines the importance of spending time with God and getting to know him. The more we know of God, the more we will be able to trust him.

Finally, we are urged to be still before the Lord and wait patiently. I find it interesting that stillness is often associated with strength in the Bible, for example, 'In quietness and trust is your strength' (Isaiah 30:15); 'Those who wait on the Lord shall renew *their* strength (Isaiah 40:31, NKJV). What might we miss if we neglect to take the time to be still in his presence?

Twice more we are told not to fret (vv. 7–8). Worry and anger will only bring us harm. They are the opposites of delighting in God and waiting patiently for him. When we trust in God and do good, when we focus our minds on his blessings and let him work in our hearts, we find we have a sure foundation to face the world.

Father, as I quiet myself before you, help me to know you better and to see where I need to trust you more. Amen.

JACKIE HARRIS

Trust in God's promises

A little while, and the wicked will be no more; though you look for them, they will not be found. But the meek will inherit the land and enjoy peace and prosperity. (vv. 10–11, NIV)

Some people always turn to the end of a book before starting it. If they like the ending, they will read the story. I've never quite understood that, but I do appreciate David's tactic in these verses. He is reminding the people how their story will end. It might look like those who have turned their backs on God are winning, but the truth is that they are on borrowed time. However things may appear, God's people have a wonderful inheritance to look forward to, whereas the evildoers have no future at all.

Look at the contrasts David describes. The wicked will one day disappear, never to return (v. 10), they will face God's judgement (v. 13), their own weapons will be used against them (v. 15), they will lose their power (v. 17) and, ultimately, they will perish completely (v. 20).

The righteous, however, can look forward to peace and prosperity (v. 11), they will know God's care (v. 17), they have an inheritance that will endure forever (v. 18) and they will flourish even in hard times (v. 19).

David is driving home his message that God's people have security. Living God's way brings peace, fulfilment and a glorious future. They can know his blessing, provision and care both now and eternally.

Perhaps we, too, need to remind ourselves of the big picture. It might appear as though things are spiralling out of control, but God is working his purposes out. We have not only his promises but also his presence with us through Jesus. Our lives are rooted and built up in him (Colossians 2:6–7) and nothing can separate us from his love (Romans 8:37–39).

Father, thank you for the reminder that we are secure in you and that goodness will triumph. Help us to persevere and to grow in courage and faith as we seek to live for you. Amen.

JACKIE HARRIS

Know that God is with you

The Lord directs the steps of the godly. He delights in every detail of their lives. Though they stumble, they will never fall, for the Lord holds them by the hand. (vv. 23–24, NLT)

Having reminded the people of God's promises, David now reminds them of God's care and provision. Their security is based not simply on promises for the future but on the day-to-day guidance, attention and protection they experience from God. Whatever is happening around them, God knows and is alongside them (vv. 23–24).

This is a precious truth to hold on to when it seems like the bad things are winning. Perhaps you need to be reminded that God is with you today. Whatever is pressing in on your mind, God knows. Whatever you are struggling with, God knows. Whether you are weeping or rejoicing, God knows. We might feel like we are just stumbling along, but these verses assure us that God won't let us fall if we put our trust in him.

Do you remember the wonderful song, 'The Blessing', sung online by representatives from over 65 churches and Christian movements at the height of the Covid pandemic? It was a reminder that God was with us in the frightening situation we faced. It was also an example of God's people responding generously to those around them, sharing their hope and seeking to bring peace to troubled hearts.

David indicates that generosity should be the hallmark of God's people (v. 21) and he gives testimony from his own experience (vv. 25–26). He says he has seen first-hand how God has provided for his people and witnessed how God's people have responded by sharing with others. They live differently because they recognise God's care and provision for them.

Spend a few moments thinking about God's knowledge of and care for you. In what ways are you seeing his provision? How might you respond?

Father, thank you that you know every detail of my life. Help me to recognise your provision for me today and give me a generous heart towards others. Amen.

JACKIE HARRIS

Live to please him

The mouths of the righteous utter wisdom, and their tongues speak what is just. The law of their God is in their hearts; their feet do not slip. (vv. 30–31, NIV)

We're continuing with the thought that God's people are called to live lives that honour him. According to David, in response to God's care, God's people should be careful in pleasing him. David outlines three ways we can do this.

First, we pay attention to what we do (v. 27). It's easy to look around and criticise what is happening, but what are we doing to make things different? Might we even be contributing to a problem by our actions or inaction? We are called to do good in any way we can: 'Let your light shine before others, that they may see your good deeds and glorify your Father in heaven' (Matthew 5:16). What might that look like for you today?

Second, we pay attention to what we say (v. 30). Do we speak wisely and honestly or join in with criticism and gossip? Paul counsels: 'Do not let any unwholesome talk come out of your mouths, but only what is helpful for building others up according to their needs, that it may benefit those who listen' (Ephesians 4:29).

Third, we are to spend time studying God's word, letting it take root in our hearts so it can change us from the inside out and guide us (v. 31). Perhaps we could pray with the psalmist: 'Teach me, Lord, the way of your decrees, that I may follow it to the end. Give me understanding, so that I may keep your law and obey it with all my heart' (Psalm 119:33–34).

There's well-known phrase, 'Be the change you wish to see in the world.' Try to monitor what you are doing, saying and thinking about over the next few days. Are you reflecting God's goodness to the world?

Pray the Lord's Prayer slowly, letting each line inspire a prayer for a situation that concerns you in the world, in your community or in your own life.

JACKIE HARRIS

Keep a steady course

Put your hope in the Lord. Travel steadily along his path. He will honour you by giving you the land. You will see the wicked destroyed. (v. 34, NLT)

We come now to what is perhaps the most challenging of all the things David counsels the righteous to do – to simply keep on keeping on. For the fifth time in this psalm, David reminds the people of their inheritance and for the fifth and sixth times, he asserts that the wicked are doomed. In the meantime, however, there are three wise pieces of advice to follow.

First, a recognition that life will not be easy (vv. 32–33). David has been reminding people of God's wonderful promises, but he recognised that this didn't mean they could expect an easy ride. There would be opposition and difficulty. Jesus says something very similar: 'In this world you will have trouble. But take heart! I have overcome the world' (John 16:33, NIV).

Second, we need to keep a steady course (v. 34). I have deliberately chosen to quote today's verse from the New Living Translation because it speaks to me of perseverance, of quietly following God's ways no matter what is happening around us. It also reminds me of Jesus' invitation to those who are weary to take on his yoke (Matthew 11:28–29). What a comfort to recognise and remember that we don't travel alone.

Finally, we are encouraged to notice those doing good (vv. 37–38). What are you focusing on today? The media would have us focus on everything that is going wrong, and that can really pull us down. We need to balance that by taking note of the good we see around us. Paul tells the Philippian church to focus on what is true, admirable, good and praiseworthy (Philippians 4:8). Let's intentionally try to do that today.

Father, thank you that the future is in your hands. Help me to keep a steady course, and to be among those known for being honest and good. Amen.

JACKIE HARRIS

All will be well

The salvation of the righteous comes from the Lord; he is their stronghold in time of trouble. The Lord helps them and delivers them; he delivers them from the wicked and saves them, because they take refuge in him. (vv. 39–40, NIV)

David ends his sermon with a reminder that God offers safety and security to his people not only in the future but also in the present. Look at the words he uses: God saves, he helps, he rescues, he is a fortress – a shelter where his people can find safety.

These images of God as a fortress or shelter are ones David uses in many of his psalms. He presents God as a refuge, a safe place, a place his people can go to when they are afraid. When life becomes overwhelming, when it appears that evil has the upper hand, David says we can trust God and find refuge in him. But do we?

Like the people of Israel who often sought refuge in foreign gods, man-made idols or ill-advised alliances, we, too, might seek comfort from other things when we feel worried or upset. For us, it might be seeking refuge in daydreams, comfort eating, shopping or something else. If we're honest, where is our place of refuge? Who or what do we turn to first when life appears to come at us from all directions?

David never answers the question about why wickedness seems to prosper, but throughout this psalm he offers wise advice about how to maintain our hope. He urges his listeners to focus on God, to recognise his care and his presence with them and to trust him for the future. He counsels them to pay attention to what they say and do, to be faithful and to seek refuge in God.

In an earlier psalm, David writes: 'The Lord is the stronghold of my life' (Psalm 27:1). May we learn to make God our stronghold as we seek to live out our faith in an imperfect world.

Give thanks to God that he has saved us and continues to help us, rescue us and keep us safe.

JACKIE HARRIS

The names of God

Chine McDonald writes:

What's in a name? Anyone who has ever had the task of naming a child – or even a pet – will know the weight of responsibility that comes with choosing a name. In the case of naming children, the sense of responsibility comes when you realise that they will have to carry that name around with them their whole lives.

I know when my husband and I were naming our children, we wanted names that would carry meaning. Names that would symbolise who we were as a family, our history, our heritage, our identity and our beliefs about the world. Names can tell you so much about a person. Our first son is named after a political figure in history that perhaps betrays how his parents might vote. Our second son has a strong Old Testament name, but we know that like every character in the Bible, our son's namesake had his flaws. But what about God's names?

According to some estimates, there are more than 900 names used for God in the Bible; and it feels like this is deliberate. The Bible is full of stories and accounts of human beings and their encounters with God. The stories told about God in scripture each reflect a different aspect of God's attributes and personality. Each encounter with God tells us something about God and about those having the encounter. God is the Almighty, the Banner, the Shepherd, the Provider, the Master. God is Everlasting and Jealous, the Lord of Hosts. God is our Peace. I have been struck by how the English language is so limiting when it comes to describing who God is. When we delve deeper into the Hebrew, Greek and Aramaic origins of certain names for God, we find a richness and a real insight into what is intended by the use of those particular names.

Whichever name is used for God, the overwhelming narrative that runs through the whole of scripture is that God loves us and wants to be in relationship with us. God is present at the beginning and at the end, through the ups and downs that life throws at us. God's faithfulness to us is worthy to be praised. So, as we read in Psalm 148:13: 'Let them praise the name of the Lord, for his name alone is exalted; his splendour is above the earth and the heavens' (NIV).

In the beginning

In the beginning God created the heavens and the earth. Now the earth was formless and empty, darkness was over the surface of the deep, and the Spirit of God was hovering over the waters. (vv. 1–2, NIV)

This is where we begin; at the start of it all. The formation of the world. Here is our introduction to who God is. He is the Creator who, a little later on in Genesis, will breathe life into humankind. Here we read the first name for God: *Elohim*. *Elohim* is the name of God found in Genesis 1 before the writer switches to the name *Yahweh* in Genesis 2. In Genesis 1, the Hebrew word *Elohim* denotes God in the plural, highlighting God in three persons: the Trinity. Here, it is established right from the start that the one true God is Father, Son and Holy Spirit, and the three in one was present right from the foundation of the earth.

In the books and chapters to come, we will read of other names of God that highlight God's nature and characteristics. But today, we meditate on the creation story and God's identity and presence at the beginning of it all. God is the source of all creativity, bringing forth something wonderful out of nothing. This God is the all-powerful, creative one, whose Spirit hovers over the waters. God created and sustains the heavens and the earth. Not just then, but even now and in the times that are to come. *Elohim* does not just sustain the earth, but for us as individuals, God is the source of our breath. He sustains our lives, too. A simple reflection on the opening verses of Genesis 1 is a reminder for each of us today of where we begin.

Creator God, thank you that in you we live and move and have our being. May we feel the breath of God hovering over our lives today. In the name of the Father, Son and Holy Spirit. Amen.

CHINE MCDONALD

The Lord is there

'And the name of the city from that time on will be: the Lord is there.'
(v. 35, NIV)

In his new year sermon in 1891, the well-known preacher and theologian Charles Spurgeon said of the closing words of the book of Ezekiel about the holy city of Jerusalem: 'It is esteemed by the prophet to be the highest blessing that could come upon a city that its name should be, *Jehovah-Shammah*, the Lord is there.'

The final passage of Ezekiel 48 details prophecies about the gates of the new city of Jerusalem, while the previous chapters include descriptions of the ideal temple. There are lots of architectural details, lots of talk of walls, paths, doors and cubits. The writer of Ezekiel goes to great lengths to explain the structure of what is being built in this holy place. I'm reminded of some of the most beautifully designed cities I've visited: from Paris to Singapore to Sydney. But as Charles Spurgeon said over a century ago, the holy city is not just another architectural feat. Jerusalem is the holy city in which God dwells, and this is the highest blessing that can be bestowed upon any place.

As Christians, we believe that our bodies are temples of the Holy Spirit, that God dwells within us. We move from an understanding of God as inhabiting a physical place that can only be approached by those serving as priests, to the beautiful understanding of the veil having been torn in two and God dwelling 'here', not just somewhere else. The wonderful truth about *Jehovah-Shammah* is that the Lord is 'there' really means the Lord is right here. For God's chosen people, who had felt distant from God exiled in Babylonia, this promised future described by Ezekiel brings profound comfort. In *Jehovah-Shammah*, they have a God who never leaves or forsakes them.

Ever-present God, thank you that you dwell right here with us. Thank you that we do not need to go to special buildings or build great temples to house your Spirit. Thank you for your presence with us always. In Jesus' name. Amen.

CHINE MCDONALD

The Lord is my banner

And Moses built an altar and called it, The Lord is my banner. He said, 'A hand upon the banner of the Lord! The Lord will have war with Amalek from generation to generation.' (vv. 15–16, NRSV)

If you're a little like me, you can glaze over when the Old Testament goes into great detail about military battles. I tend to do the same in long battle or fight scenes in some of the most iconic films and TV shows such as *The Lord of the Rings* and *Game of Thrones*. It can be hard to grasp what these epic stories of war and conflict are really trying to tell us. Today's passage is a reminder of who our God is and the impact that who he is has on the battles we face in daily life. It describes the altar Moses builds to celebrate the Israelites beating the Amalekites at Rephidim.

During this battle, Moses stood at a vantage point and held the staff of God in his arms. As long as Moses' hands were held aloft, Israel had the advantage over the Amalekites. When Moses' arms grew weary, his brother Aaron and another man named Hur came to his aid and held Moses' arms up for him. This unusual battle victory – which showed God was with the Israelites and it was not just about their own military strength – was worth remembering, so Moses built an altar to mark it, naming it 'The Lord is my banner'.

Although most of us may never find ourselves in military battle, we can find deep truth in the idea of God as our 'banner'. Many of us will be familiar with flags or symbols that mark our belonging to a particular group. Whatever battles we are going through in life, may we today be encouraged and reminded about who we are and who our God is: the God who walks with us in battle and makes us victorious.

Jehovah-Nissi, thank you that your presence goes with us into every situation that life throws at us. Help us today to be reminded of that presence and to feel you with us. In Jesus' name. Amen.

CHINE MCDONALD

The I am

God said to Moses, 'I am who I am. This is what you are to say to the Israelites: "I am has sent me to you."' (v. 14, NIV)

What image is conjured up in your mind when you hear the word 'God'? The 2021 UK Census results showed that fewer people are ticking the 'Christian' box than ever before. Meanwhile, the past decade has seen a significant rise in the number of people from other religions, including Islam, Hinduism, Sikhism and many other smaller faiths. When some think of the word 'God', they may be thinking of a completely different being to the one we as Christians worship.

Today's passage reminds me of Acts 17 in which Paul is at the Areopagus and trying to convince a diverse group of religious people that the gods they worship do not compare to the one true God – the one in whom we 'live and move and have our being' (Acts 17:28). The God we serve is unrivalled and unmatched – the source of all, the most high God.

In today's passage, in response to Moses asking how he should introduce the Israelites to God, God says: 'I am who I am.' Young people today might rephrase this as: 'I am God. End of.' God is the beginning and the end; he needs no explanation or introduction. He is the God who has been with them all along, throughout history, and will be forevermore.

At times I can become so familiar with God that I lose the sense of awe and wonder at his omnipotence and awesomeness. When speaking about my Christian faith to others, I can feel self-conscious rather than boldly proclaiming that God is God. End of. May I have the boldness to introduce others to the great 'I am'.

God of all, we pray for our friends and family who do not know you. We pray for opportunities to introduce them to who you are. In Jesus' name. Amen.

CHINE MCDONALD

God, our provider

Abraham looked up and there in a thicket he saw a ram caught by its horns. He went over and took the ram and sacrificed it as a burnt offering instead of his son. So Abraham called that place The Lord Will Provide. And to this day it is said, 'On the mountain of the Lord it will be provided.' (vv. 13–14, NIV)

A friend recently told me that she often prays aloud for a parking space when she goes to the shops; and sometimes it's while her toddler is in the car. She does it so often that she is concerned that God will be reduced in her child's eyes to the provider of parking spaces. When we talk about God being our provider, it can be difficult for us to think beyond the material. So often I have heard people talk of God's provision through examples like the arrival of a surprise income or the delivery of a passport or a house or a car. But God's provision of course goes much deeper than that. If we believe that God is omnipotent, then God can do far more than we can ask or imagine.

Today's reading tells the story of Abraham being tested by God. Asked to sacrifice his son Isaac on the altar, Abraham agrees to do so, but as he takes up the knife to slay his son, God stops him. God says that Abraham has demonstrated that he fears God because Abraham has not withheld his only son. This can be a difficult story to reconcile with the idea of a loving God most of us have. But what is striking in this account is that Abraham trusts so completely in God that he knows even before it happens that 'God himself will provide the lamb for the burnt offering' (v. 8). This goes beyond the immediate provision of the sacrificial lamb. It looks to the future, hundreds of years later, when God provided Jesus – his own Son – to be the ultimate sacrifice, the ultimate provision.

What difference will Jesus's sacrifice on the cross make to your life today? How might you show your thanks for God's provision in your life?

CHINE MCDONALD

The one who sees me

She gave this name to the Lord who spoke to her: 'You are the God who sees me,' for she said, 'I have now seen the One who sees me.' (v. 13, NIV)

Today is International Women's Day, and an appropriate day to reflect on Hagar as the only person in the Bible to give God a name. Sometimes the greatest theological insight comes from the most unexpected places – the truths about who God is spoken from the downtrodden and forgotten in society.

The story of Hagar is one of the most tragic in the Bible, but ultimately also one of the most hopeful – in which the nature and character of God's kingdom is revealed. Bought as a slave and used by Abraham and Sarah, Hagar is subject to physical and sexual violence and used to give the childless couple a son: Ishmael. Hagar's experience of oppression and subjugation is tragic, but sadly, not unique. According to the World Health Organisation, one in three women worldwide today have been subjected to either physical and/or sexual intimate violence in their lifetime. Millions of women are sold into slavery around the world and there are probably women in your community or even your church who feel that they are unseen, unloved and invisible. Perhaps you yourself experience this. How wonderful it is to know that God sees us for who we are – not as broken, but as beloved children of God.

Despite not being a man or a patriarch, Hagar receives a covenant blessing directly from God about her future offspring. She receives a full birth annunciation, being told that she will give birth to a child, a precursor to Mary's annunciation and the foretelling of the birth of Jesus. Hagar is the only person in the Bible to name God. This tells us so much about the kingdom of God: a place where the powerless find power in God, a place where the weak find their strength in God, a place where the unseen are truly seen by God, *El Roi*.

God who sees us, thank you that we are fearfully and wonderfully made. Thank you that we are fiercely loved by you, no matter whether the world shows us love. Help us to see others as you see them today. Amen.

CHINE MCDONALD

Abba, Father

The Spirit you received does not make you slaves, so that you live in fear again; rather, the Spirit you received brought about your adoption to sonship. And by him we cry, '*Abba*, Father.' (v. 15, NIV)

Few things compare to the first time I heard my eldest son call me 'mummy', and my heart expands a little when I hear him refer to my husband as 'daddy'. These childlike sounds symbolise our closeness, our intimacy. As my son has grown and gone to primary school, he has gradually picked up the idea that big boys have 'mums' and 'dads' – not 'mummies' and 'daddies'. I want him to keep calling us mummy and daddy for as long as possible. There is a slight distance that comes with the word 'dad'. Dad feels one step closer than 'father', but 'daddy' refers to that closeness between a child and their parent – the dependence, the trust and the love. One reading of the word 'Abba' is 'daddy'.

Today's passage is one of the most foundational to Christian understanding of salvation. Paul writes of the special access to God granted to us through the Spirit. Through the Holy Spirit, we are no longer slaves but have been brought into God's family – not as visitors, but as treasured members who have an intimate relationship with God the Father. This adoption does not mean that things will always go our way, or that our lives will be free of suffering. Instead, in all of life's ups and downs, we know that we have a Father in heaven who will always be with us, holding our hand through it all.

I'm reminded of this every time my son cries out for me or his dad when he is hurt: the intimate call to someone who loves you with an everlasting love. What a privilege it is for us to be invited into God's family through what Jesus did for us on the cross, making it possible for us to cry, '*Abba*, Father.'

Abba, Father, thank you that you invite us into your family, no matter who we are. May we live in the light of your glorious salvation. Through Jesus Christ our Lord. Amen.

CHINE MCDONALD

God, our peace

The Lord said to him, 'Peace! Do not be afraid. You are not going to die.' So Gideon built an altar to the Lord there and called it The Lord Is Peace. To this day it stands in Ophrah of the Abiezrites. (vv. 23–24, NIV)

The English Puritan preacher Thomas Watson said: 'If God be our God, he will give us peace in trouble. When there is a storm without, he will make peace within.' I love the straightforwardness of these words; the unwavering assurance that God is our peace. There are moments when I feel the same – an overwhelming sense of peace; a peace which can only come from God. But, if I'm honest, most of the time, I do not feel at peace. There are the daily grinds and frustrations that cause anger and resentment. There are the to-do lists that keep us awake at night. There are the news headlines that tell tales of disaster, conflict and misery. The past few years have been relentless – the pandemic, the cost-of-living crisis, political turbulence and more have robbed us of peace.

In today's passage, Gideon panics when he sees the angel of the Lord face to face. The exclamation marks in the passage show Gideon's sense of alarm. If you're anything like me, then you might know that feeling. An anxious feeling that rises in the pit of your tummy when you realise something is wrong, or simply the gnawing creep of uneasiness about the state of your life or the state of the world. God's response to Gideon's panic is simple: 'Peace!' God tells Gideon not to be afraid, and apparently the panic subsides and peace sets in. Gideon builds an altar to commemorate what has happened. His altar is a reminder not of the advantage of slowing our breathing or practising positive thinking to alleviate our fears and anxieties, but that God is the one who is our peace, no matter what is happening around us.

God, our peace, forgive us when we have panicked or been anxious about the state of the world. Thank you that your Holy Spirit gives us a peace that passes understanding, even in the midst of it all. Amen.

CHINE MCDONALD

Ancient of Days

'As I looked, thrones were set in place, and the Ancient of Days took his seat. His clothing was as white as snow; the hair of his head was white like wool. His throne was flaming with fire, and its wheels were all ablaze.' (v. 9, NIV)

We live in a world that values youth. We have long heard about the quest to stave off the ageing process, to pursue the elixir of youth. In job interviews, those who are younger are deemed more energetic, innovative and creative, their brain cells more functioning. I have heard of many middle-aged and older people having to send off hundreds of CVs in search of jobs. It seems in the workplace – just as in other spaces, including the entertainment and music industries – there is a bias against older people.

In church settings, older people can often feel sidelined and forgotten, their needs ignored in a world where bringing in younger generations is a priority. But all of us miss out when we lose the wisdom of older generations. There are some communities around the world where age is valued, where the elders of a tribe or village are revered. This is true in my own community among the Igbo in Nigeria, for example. With age comes a profound wisdom.

In today's passage, God is described as the Ancient of Days – not only in the sense that God has been there since the beginning of time, but that he looks like it too! He takes the form of an old man, wearing clothes as white as snow and with hair like pure wool. This striking image of an immortal God, who was before and is and ever shall be, might help us to see the beauty that comes with age, the transcendent knowing of a God who is immortal.

Today, may we find space to praise the 'Immortal, invisible, God only wise', as the great hymn goes: 'Most blessed, most glorious, the Ancient of Days; almighty, victorious, thy great name we praise.'

Ancient of Days, we lift our hearts in praise to you. Thank you that you were there in the beginning, you are and will be to come. May we find strength and peace by resting in your everlasting arms. Amen.

CHINE MCDONALD

Most High God

Whoever dwells in the shelter of the Most High will rest in the shadow of the Almighty. I will say of the Lord, 'He is my refuge and my fortress, my God, in whom I trust.' (vv. 1–2, NIV)

Not long after the death of Queen Victoria in 1901, a newspaper article was published which revealed that the queen had a living Christian faith. Once, after listening to a sermon, she told the speaker that she wished Jesus would return in her lifetime. He asked her why that was so, and she replied: 'I should like to lay my crown at his feet.' There is something profound about imagining an earthly ruler or monarch humbling themselves before the Most High God.

The death of Queen Elizabeth II in 2022 highlighted her late majesty's deep faith in Jesus Christ, and we also witnessed the sheer enormity of the death of a monarch who was sovereign over the UK and, at certain other points in history, sovereign over many nations. Earthly kingdoms, however, are nothing in comparison to the heavenly kingdom of the Most High God.

I remember hearing stories of the instructions given to those who were going to meet Queen Elizabeth. There were rules about how to address her, how to curtsey or bow, how to say goodbye, how to speak to her and how not to. All were designed to keep a sense of distance and a sense of reverence when it came to being in the presence of the queen. We saw much of that remain in her death, with thousands of people queueing for hours – or even days – to file past her coffin.

As Christians, we are given special access to the Most High; and the even more amazing thing is that this King runs towards us with open arms. The Most High does not keep us at a distance. Through the incarnation, God becomes just like us, stepping into our messiness and walking alongside us through the ups and downs of life.

Most High God, thank you for your great love for us. Thank you that our sins are washed away. May we never lose the wonder of this truth. May we never lose the wonder of who you are and what you have done for us. Amen.

CHINE MCDONALD

God, our healer

He said, 'If you listen carefully to the Lord your God and do what is right in his eyes, if you pay attention to his commands and keep all his decrees, I will not bring on you any of the diseases I brought on the Egyptians, for I am the Lord, who heals you.' (v. 26, NIV)

The gospel accounts are full of stories of Jesus healing people – from blind Bartimaeus (Mark 10:46–52) to Jairus' daughter (Matthew 9:18–26) to the woman with the chronic bleeding (Luke 8:43–48). Critics of Christianity claim that no one can defy the rules of science, but we believe in a God who can not only defy natural laws, but who is also the source of all that exists – the beginning and the end.

Throughout history, miraculous healings have been a significant part of Christian faith. Healing symbolises the power of God over earthly things, but when it comes to healing from afflictions, medical conditions or illnesses, it can signify God's love for us. Although physical healing sometimes does not happen, we believe in a God who heals (*Jehovah Rapha*). Today's reading reminds us of that. But God is not just a healer of physical conditions. The Bible is full of stories of restoration and repair, of making whole and making right. God invites us to be part of the repair and restoration; the healing of a fallen and broken world – physically, spiritually and materially.

I recently came across the concept of *Tikkun olam* in the Jewish tradition – the act of repairing and improving the world, returning to its originally intended divine beauty. We often speak about the idea of *shalom* – wholeness, completeness, harmony – and pray that God's *shalom* peace might be restored in this world. God is the God who heals; able to heal our physical pain and afflictions, but in so doing reminding us that one day all things in heaven and earth will be made new.

As you meditate on today's passage, be attentive to what in your home, your family, your community, your church or your nation needs God's healing today. Pray that Jehovah Rapha would restore and make whole.

CHINE MCDONALD

The God of the house of God

There he built an altar, and he called the place El Bethel, because it was there that God revealed himself to him when he was fleeing from his brother. (v. 7, NIV)

Do you have a pet name for someone? Perhaps a friend or a relative or a child or a spouse? Pet names often playfully relate to a past memory, an old story that connects you and that person together, often with a knowing smile. Pet names denote relationship and shared history and encounter. In Genesis 28, a few chapters before today's reading, Jacob renamed the city of Luz, Bethel – meaning 'house of God' – after he had a dream in which he saw a stairway or ladder that stretched all the way to heaven. Many years later, after experiencing the trauma of his daughter Dinah being raped and his sons taking revenge by going on a killing spree, Jacob is told by God to return to Bethel. He builds another altar as a marker of what God did there, calling it *El Bethel*, because it was there that God had originally been revealed.

For Jacob, *El Bethel* was a personal name that he had for God: a pet name, perhaps. Jacob is the only one who uses this name for God, reflecting the personal relationship that they had. Jacob knows who God is. By telling Jacob to return to Bethel and reminding Jacob that God is the God of the house of God – the same God Jacob had had an encounter with previously – God shows Jacob that he is never alone. God is always with him and always has been. They have history – a history in which God has seen him through some of the most trying and difficult times of his life. It's good to be reminded that the God of the house of God will never leave us nor forsake us.

Where in your life do you need a reminder that God is with you always? Spend time in God's presence, being reminded of God's promises through the good times and the bad.

CHINE MCDONALD

God with us

'Therefore the Lord himself will give you a sign: the virgin will conceive and give birth to a son, and will call him Immanuel.' (v. 14, NIV)

Today's passage feels so familiar because it is one of those passages we often hear read aloud during Advent. Here, the prophecy looks forward to the birth of Jesus. We have been reflecting on the names of God, but at the heart of our faith is the beautiful truth that God Almighty came down to earth, taking the form of a helpless baby. The incarnation powerfully demonstrates to us that the Father and the Son, along with the Holy Spirit, are one. God steps into our broken world, with all its mess, conflict, hatred, emptiness and hopelessness and stands alongside us in it. The wonder of our faith is that God loves us enough to do that.

Throughout the Bible, we see a God who is both near and far, ever-present and yet also omnipotent. A holy and awesome God, but also the Holy Spirit who dwells within us. God is not distant, and through Jesus, he breaks the curse of sin and death, bringing light where there is darkness and hope where there is despair. God is not a spectator watching our movements and judging us from the firmament, but here with us right now. In the middle of some of the darkest moments of our lives, what a comfort it is to know that. When the healing doesn't come soon enough; when the dark clouds brood over our minds; when we face hardships; when the world seems a scary place and we fear for the future, God is right there with us. God hasn't abandoned us or forsaken us. Instead, God has come right alongside us. God is with us. Immanuel.

Immanuel, thank you that you do not leave us or forsake us, that your presence is with us no matter where we go. Today, may we find moments to feel a sense of your presence with us. Help us to hear you above the noise. Amen.
CHINE MCDONALD

Alpha and Omega

'Look, I am coming soon! My reward is with me, and I will give to each person according to what they have done. I am the Alpha and the Omega, the First and the Last, the Beginning and the End.'
(vv. 12–13, NIV)

It feels appropriate to end our time together with a reflection on one of the most-used names for God: the Alpha and the Omega, the First and the Last, the Beginning and the End. Today's passage, found at the end of the Bible, looks forward to a day in which Christ returns and judges the whole earth. But what strikes me is that he has been there all along. Right from the foundations of the earth in which the Spirit of God was hovering over the waters, right through the journey out of Eden to Israel's enslavement and exodus, through the chosen people's rollercoaster of encounters with God – through burning bushes and parted seas, through wars and fallen kings and faith-filled women.

He was there in the beginning – 'the Word was with God, and the Word was God' (John 1:1) – through the miraculous encounters with people just like you and me, through the pain and torment and glory of the crucifixion and the resurrection and ascension, through to the great acts of a church on fire for Jesus, through to the vision of Revelation. God – Father, Son and Holy Spirit – has been there through it all. God does not pop in and out of history, occasionally checking in on us to see how we are doing. God has been right there through it all – beside us through it all.

What a comfort it is to know that God was not just present *at* the beginning and the end but *is* the beginning and the end. May we live in the light of God's presence in us. May we speak the truth about what God has done and, in so doing, draw others to light, love, forgiveness and wholeness.

Eternal God, who are we that you are mindful of us? We praise you for your everlasting love, your never-ending presence and your constant compassion towards us. May we never lose the wonder of the glory of your name. Amen.
CHINE MCDONALD

Hosea: God's redeeming love (part 1)

Helen Williams writes:

Apart from delighting in some of its reassuring verses about God's love, I confess I have paid little attention to Hosea over the years. Even finding him among the other eleven minor prophets can be a challenge! Having discovered (and wept through) the novel *Redeeming Love* by Francine Rivers (Multnomah, 1997) – which adds a gripping 464 pages of flesh to the bones of Hosea's own marriage story – I assumed I now completely understood Hosea. In reality, the story of Hosea's marriage to the prostitute, Gomer, occupies only part of the first three chapters of Hosea. There are a further eleven chapters, making for some challenging reading. It may be challenging but it is worth trying to read through the whole of this astonishing book. It should only take about 30 minutes, and it would give you a great overview before we dive into some of the themes.

You'll find there's an opening verse (1:1) from the book's compiler, setting it in its historical context, and a closing verse (14:9) placing it firmly in whatever context you, the reader, find yourself – in other words, its message is utterly relevant for today. Chapters 1—3 contain the story of Hosea himself, with God's instruction to marry Gomer and to stay faithful to her, come what may. This is followed by two sets of accusations and warnings for Israel (chapters 4—11 and 12—14), each of which concludes (thankfully!) with a poem full of God's mercy and of hope for the future. This tension between judgement and mercy is the essence of the book.

Hosea's own name comes from the same Hebrew root as that of Joshua, meaning 'salvation'. This anthology of some 25 years of his prophetic preaching is all about this very thing. God's chosen people entered into a covenant with him in the Sinai desert but repeatedly broke it, disobeying his commandments and falling into waywardness and idolatry. We see God's heart for his people utterly broken; the inevitable judgement that has to come; and (spoiler alert!) that he can only be true to who he is, the God of love. He cannot not be merciful! From our post-New Testament vantage point, we know that ultimately, the only answer to deserved judgement for all people would be for Jesus to give his own life. Hints at the one who is to come are woven through these prophecies.

You cannot be serious!

When the Lord began to speak through Hosea, the Lord said to him, 'Go, marry a promiscuous woman and have children with her, for like an adulterous wife this land is guilty of unfaithfulness to the Lord.' So he married Gomer daughter of Diblaim. (vv. 2–3, NIV)

After Solomon's death, the twelve tribes of Israel split into two kingdoms. Judah and Benjamin formed the Southern Kingdom of Judah with its capital Jerusalem, and the remaining tribes became the Northern Kingdom – Israel (or Ephraim), ruled from its capital, Samaria. Two hundred years later, somewhere between 753 and 729BC, we find Hosea living in this Northern Kingdom and we read that God 'began to speak through' him. Isaiah, Amos and Micah were also active around this time. Good kings and bad kings have come and gone, but Jeroboam II has led the people through a prosperous age. It's a tough time for a prophet to speak of sin and judgement, but with Jeroboam's death things start to unravel and the fall of this dynasty is imminent. Prosperity has led to spiritual complacency, and this to serious infidelity.

The book opens with God's extraordinary command to Hosea to find and marry Gomer, known for her promiscuity. Some commentators think she may even have been a cult prostitute, a follower of Baal worship with its many fertility rites.

Can you imagine what Hosea thought when God asked this of him? He must have wondered if he'd heard God correctly. He must have been terrified for his reputation. What about his hopes and dreams of love, a good and godly wife and a happy family? We don't know how long he waited before answering God but there is no suggestion that he did anything other than jump up, go and find Gomer and marry her immediately. We can only wonder what her reaction was too!

All this because God needed Hosea to speak to his people from the depths of his own heart, with authenticity, with empathy, with the desperate knowledge of how it feels to be spurned and rejected.

'Every revelation of God is a demand, and the way to knowledge of God is obedience,' wrote William Temple. We obey when we trust. Dare we pray for ears like Hosea's to hear God and an ability like his to trust and obey?

HELEN WILLIAMS

What's in a name?

Gomer conceived again and gave birth to a daughter. Then the Lord said to Hosea, 'Call her Lo-Ruhamah (which means "not loved"), for I will no longer show love to Israel.' (v. 6, NIV)

Two days ago, it was my birthday – a celebration of the day I became Helen. My name's not fashionable anymore but I have always loved that it means 'light' and my middle name, Ruth, means 'friend'. I often pray to live true to my name. Last year, before my first grandchild was born, the whole family spent hours discussing what he would be called, amid cries of 'You can't call him that!'

In today's reading, we hear of three children who were given, under God's instruction, what appear to be the most awful names. I wonder how those children coped with their names, once they were old enough to play with others.

Jezreel, the eldest, has a name synonymous with 'bloodshed'. It harks back to the dreadful massacre of King Ahab's family by Jehu at Naboth's vineyard (2 Kings 10). God had not forgotten the cruelty, injustice and ambition of this attack. Punishment was overdue.

Second, came a daughter – 'not loved' was the meaning of her name, for she was to be a symbol to the people of the fact that God was withdrawing his love from his people.

When little Not Loved was weaned (probably at the age of two), her mum gave birth to another child, a child with a name showing God's determination to disown his people forever – 'not my people'. It seems hard to us, reading this now, to think of this little family with its terrible reputation and the blood-chilling names. God had tried everything to woo his people back to him – it was time for desperate measures.

In Revelation 2:17, God promises a new name to those who follow him. Why not spend some time thinking about your own name and asking God what his name for you is? Your identity in him is all.

HELEN WILLIAMS

My loved one

'Yet the Israelites will be like the sand on the seashore, which cannot be measured or counted. In the place where it was said to them, "You are not my people," they will be called "children of the living God"'. **(v. 10, NIV)**

If you ever saw the film *The Prince of Egypt*, you will remember the extraordinary way the Red Sea parted into a dry pathway, with huge walls of water on either side, in which you could see a myriad of beautiful sea creatures! I've snorkelled in those waters, and they are truly vibrant with colour. I mention it because I know I sometimes miss the sheer miracle of the way God delivered his people from slavery. Miracle upon miracle. He rescued them because of his passionate love for them, leading them through the desert as he prepared them for life as his chosen people in the land he had promised them. At Mount Sinai he made a covenant of faithful commitment with his people, through Moses. It's a powerful and profound moment in the relationship of God with his people as he promises lifelong protection, blessing, a home and a way to live well. In response, God's people promise, 'Everything the Lord has said we will do' (Exodus 24:3).

The desert years are a complex story of bitterness, lack of trust, temptation, idolatry and reneging on this promise. Even when they finally reach the land flowing with milk and honey, the Israelites end up taking all its abundance and dedicating it to the worship of Baal. It's no wonder their Faithful Husband is agonised.

Despite what sounds like the ultimate condemnation: 'You are not my people, and I am not your God' (1:9), here we see God's compassionate remembrance of his promise to Abraham and his promise of relationship restored and covenant renewed. Not only this, but God also promises that one day the two kingdoms will be reconciled under one leader (1:11). Finally comes God's personal promise for each individual: 'Say of… your sisters, "My loved one"' (2:1)!

Wherever you feel you are with God today, hear him say to you, 'My loved one,' for that's what you most assuredly are.

HELEN WILLIAMS

Falling out

'I will punish her for the days she burned incense to the Baals; she decked herself with rings and jewellery, and went after her lovers, but me she forgot,' declares the Lord. (v. 13, NIV)

'It is a fearful thing to fall into the hands of the living God. But it is a much more fearful thing to fall out of them,' begins the powerful poem, 'The hands of God' by D.H. Lawrence. He continues: 'Save me, O God, from falling into the ungodly knowledge of myself as I am without God. Let me never know, O God, let me never know what I am or should be when I have fallen out of your hands, the hands of the living God.'

Chapter 2 of Hosea presents us with such a life – a life alienated from God after choosing to fall out of his hands. It's serious. It's bleak and, if truth be told, it's not the God I like reading about. It's talking about broken promises, deceit, sin, pride, idolatry and sheer contempt for a covenant. This is God's desperate cry to, and condemnation of, his people, but we know from what comes next in chapter 3 that Hosea himself must have been living through a similar marital hell.

In his warning, God takes Israel back to her birth (v. 2) – the moment when she officially became his at Sinai – threatening to let her return to how she was before and lose the precious identity he has given her. In his desperation he threatens to 'block her path with thorn bushes' and 'wall her in' (v. 6), as if he is trying to save her from herself. I wonder if you've ever known God do that with you, almost wrapping you up and holding you close to his heart so you don't harm yourself or do something you'll regret. God gave his people not only identity but also gifts for a thriving life – his pain at her forgetfulness is palpable: 'She has not acknowledged that I was the one' (v. 8) and 'me she forgot' (v. 13).

O God, I so often forget to acknowledge who you are, who I am in you, where my blessings come from, how faithful you are and how much you love me. I'm so sorry. Amen.

HELEN WILLIAMS

Just deserts

'Therefore, I am now going to allure her; I will lead her into the wilderness and speak tenderly to her. There I will give her back her vineyards, and will make the Valley of Achor a door of hope'.
(vv. 14–15, NIV)

Having pursued his bride by withdrawing his blessing, God tries a different tack – luring Israel back to the beauty of their original covenant, winning her love and restoring her fortunes. The wilderness or desert might seem a strange place to take her to, but not only will this be a barren place away from distractions, but it's also the place where God and his people had known one another best, where he had daily provided for her. He will speak to her heart and woo her, and he is sure that she'll respond. The Valley of Achor means the valley of 'trouble', but God can make even this place a 'door of hope' (v. 15).

Can you think of a time (it might even be now) when God allowed you to face some trouble, leading you through your own Valley of Achor, which at the time felt desperately hard, only to find later that going through this had led you to a 'door of hope'? I love C.S. Lewis' 'Valley of the shadow of life' (*The Great Divorce*) – it's a reframing of the valley of the shadow of death in Psalm 23, a 'let's look at this in a different way', an attempt to understand with the 'eyes of our heart' what God might be doing or showing us through this time.

Sometimes we find ourselves entering a desert time and we hear God speak tenderly to us; sometimes that desert time is accompanied by a demanding silence. Waiting in that place and breathing in deep God's love for us, despite often feeling a bit confused or empty, can mean we grow and deepen in faith. I've found God often leads us to such a place ahead of a time of new ministry (think of Joseph, Moses, Elijah and especially Jesus).

I long to hear your voice, Lord, to hear your call, to be restored in your like-
ness. As I sit with you now in stillness, I ask you to breathe new life into me
and tune my heart to yours. Amen.

HELEN WILLIAMS

A marriage made in heaven

'Bow and sword and battle I will abolish from the land, so that all may lie down in safety. I will betroth you to me forever; I will betroth you in righteousness and justice, in love and compassion. I will betroth you in faithfulness, and you will acknowledge the Lord.' (vv. 18–20, NIV)

Although God has focused on going back to where they began, reminding his bride of the overwhelming love upon which their covenant was founded, there is a prophetic sense of the future in these verses. 'In that day', says Hosea three times. For us, we know that this heavenly vision of a relationship, and a world, made right will ultimately find its completion in Jesus, but Hosea could only hint at the coming Messiah.

First, to the heart of the relationship. Cunningly, Hosea uses a wordplay which would have resonated deeply with his audience, this nation who'd grown complacent, forgetting their godly identity as his chosen people and straying into serious worship of local Canaanite gods. 'Baal' means 'master' or 'lord' and Hosea makes it clear that the subservient relationship Israel has sought with the Baals falls so far short of the mutual, loving marital relationship he'd intended (vv. 16–17).

Second, he paints a picture of what her home, this promised land, should look like; of how he had designed it to be. It's a land where all is at peace. As I write, war rages in so many countries and this vision of a world at peace, as God intended it to be, is a heartbreaking and urgent prompt to pray more fervently for his reign across our world.

There is hope though! He is the God of new starts – the names he gave Hosea's children will be reversed! Even Jezreel, the 'bloodshed' boy, will be renamed 'God plants' (v. 22)! Remember 1 Peter 2:10: 'Once you were not a people, but now you are the people of God.' Notice the fruit of the Spirit in God's wooing of his people in verses 19–20 – three times he says 'I will betroth you' – it's a marriage that is to last, characterised by righteousness, justice, love, compassion and faithfulness.

Shall we pray today for a world where 'all may lie down in safety', and that many who are 'Not my people' will be compelled to turn and say, 'You are my God'?

HELEN WILLIAMS

Love with no limits

The Lord said to me, 'Go, show your love to your wife again, though she is loved by another man and is an adulteress'… So I bought her for fifteen shekels of silver and about a homer and a lethek of barley. (vv. 1–2, NIV)

In chapter 3, we return to the story of Hosea and Gomer, and I am struck by just how vulnerable Hosea is, as he speaks of the mess of his own marriage and shares God's instructions to him. I know that, as a Christian, I'm so often tempted to present myself as good, strong and capable, almost as if I think God's reputation depends on how I appear to others. Even our churches face this temptation. It's quite a reminder that God's most powerful work often happens when we are prepared to be vulnerable with others about our own mess. If 2 Corinthians 12:9 about God's power being made 'perfect in weakness' means anything, it is surely about this. So much focus in our society is on looking good, looking young, looking invincible, looking successful, but God literally brings Hosea to breaking point so his story will speak all the more powerfully to his precious people.

Not only is Hosea to love his Gomer, despite her utter rejection of him and her promiscuous lifestyle, but he is to redeem, restore and reinstate her. Buying her back (presumably doing a deal with her current lover) came at a huge cost: around 170 g of silver and 195 kg of barley! In 1 Peter 1:18–19, it says: 'For you know that it was not with perishable things such as silver or gold that you were redeemed from the empty way of life handed down to you from your ancestors, but with the precious blood of Christ.' Tomorrow, we begin the journey with Jesus through Holy Week to the cross where that blood was shed – where we ourselves were redeemed.

And here we leave Hosea for now, returning to look at the rest of the book in May.

As we come to Palm Sunday tomorrow, we pray, Lord, that you will lead us through this Holy Week captivated all over again by the depth of your unfaltering love for us, the love that cost you everything. Amen.

HELEN WILLIAMS

Jesus, the Messiah

Jane Walters writes:

When I read the Bible's accounts of Jesus' life, I often wish I'd been there at the time. Do you? How amazing it would have been to witness the miracles, listen to his words spoken by him, travel with him and enjoy his company. And then I wonder, as a writer, how I would have gone about recording those events. I wouldn't have known where to start!

Each of the gospel writers tackled this task differently. Mark's gospel is the shortest of the four and he provides a whistle-stop, action-packed narrative. Luke, the doctor, went for a more scholarly, historical account, and John, Jesus' beloved disciple, centres on the person of Jesus. So, what of Matthew's gospel, which we will be spending the next two weeks exploring?

For a start, according to commentators, we can't be sure that the author is the disciple Matthew, formerly the tax collector Levi, as we might suppose. We do know, though, that it was written somewhere between AD50 and 80, and was aimed at a Jewish audience. Most importantly, we know that the author's highest aim was to portray Jesus as the Messiah and the one to whom the entire Old Testament pointed. Time and again we read versions of his formulaic phrase, 'so was fulfilled what was said through the prophet'.

Through these 14 reflections that take us up to Easter and beyond, we will travel through well-known stories, listening out for what Matthew tells us about the Messiah. The word itself means 'anointed one' and can be interchanged with the title 'Christ'. To the Jews, this longed-for figure represented freedom and an ushering in of the kingdom of God. At the time of Jesus, the Jews were living under the oppression of Roman rule and the need for liberation was more urgent than ever. Over the generations, many false messiahs had arisen but failed to meet the demanding criteria. Now, Jesus has burst centre-stage, ticking the right boxes, but could he really be the promised Messiah?

I have consulted a range of different commentaries in my preparation for these notes and want to acknowledge that I found *The Message of Matthew* by Michael Green, in the Bible Speaks Today series (IVP, 2020), particularly helpful.

The family tree of Jesus

This is the genealogy of Jesus the Messiah the son of David, the son of Abraham: Abraham was the father of Isaac, Isaac the father of Jacob, Jacob the father of Judah and his brothers... and Jacob the father of Joseph, the husband of Mary, and Mary was the mother of Jesus who is called the Messiah. (vv. 1–2 and v. 16, NIV)

I suspect that most readers of Matthew's first chapter choose to start at verse 18, where the story *properly* begins. I know I usually do. After all, isn't the genealogy just a formality that we can skim through or ignore completely? However, in exploring this list of names, we see how the author is at pains, right from the get-go, to establish the right of Jesus to be the Messiah.

Genealogies are not uncommon in the Bible, but this one is special. The names are arranged in three groups of 14 generations, centring on the three figures of Abraham, David and Jesus. Jesus is shown to be the fulfilment of God's covenant with Abraham (that all the families of the earth would be blessed through his seed) and his covenant with David (that his throne and kingdom would be eternally established before God). In short, the author is declaring that the entire Old Testament points to Jesus.

You may have noticed that women are included in this list – most unusual for such genealogies of the time – and what a selection they are! Tamar's story (Genesis 38) is a scandalous one; Rahab was the prostitute God used to spare the two spies during the fall of Jericho (Joshua 2); Bathsheba was coerced by King David into adulterous affair (2 Samuel 11); and Ruth was a Moabite, excluded by Mosaic law from the assembly of the Lord (see Deuteronomy 23:3). As for Mary, though we know she was a virgin, the rumours surrounding her pregnancy put her in a very poor light.

It's not exactly a Hall of Fame. Instead, this genealogy reveals how God has been working his purpose out through every generation, through men and women who are flawed and failing, just as we are.

Father God, thank you for sending Jesus, the Messiah. Thank you for all the lives you've touched and used in fulfilling your promise to the world. Thank you for choosing me to be part of your purpose, too. Amen.

JANE WALTERS

What's in a name?

All this took place to fulfil what the Lord had said through the prophet: 'The virgin will conceive and give birth to a son, and they will call him Immanuel' (which means 'God with us'). (vv. 22–23, NIV)

There's a story of a young child telling her teacher that she was drawing God. Puzzled, the teacher says, 'But no one knows what God looks like.' With utter confidence, the girl replies, 'They will when I'm finished.'

One of the author's devices in writing this gospel is to draw attention to where the Old Testament is being fulfilled, and he does this here by quoting a well-known verse from Isaiah. He is saying that this baby is what the prophet said the Messiah would look like.

Although Jews had anticipated the coming of the Messiah for centuries, their image of him was as a powerful, political figure who would overthrow earthly governments and establish a new rule. What nonsense it was to be pointing to a baby! Yet in chapter 2 we read of how King Herod was shaken to his core over the news that the magi reported: the king of the Jews has been born. Herod knew better than to dismiss this tiny scrap of humanity.

So much for physical appearance. What about his name, Immanuel? In Hebrew tradition, names were full of meaning and bore great significance, speaking into a person's character or hopes for their future. Immanuel, 'God with us', was not, of course, the name the Messiah used while he lived on earth but he was called Jesus, meaning 'God saves'. Both names are connected, declaring that he will be the one who deals with the sin that separates humanity from God so that communion is restored. He promises to be with us and, because of his sacrifice, we can be with him for eternity.

Jesus, I thank you that you are the one who has saved and rescued me and that I can count on you being with me always. Reveal your presence to me now, in these quiet moments. Amen.

JANE WALTERS

The warm-up act

In those days John the Baptist came, preaching in the wilderness of Judea and saying, 'Repent, for the kingdom of heaven has come near.' This is he who was spoken of through the prophet Isaiah: 'A voice of one calling in the wilderness, "Prepare the way for the Lord, make straight paths for him."' (vv. 1–3, NIV)

We're all used to the idea of a 'warm-up'. Whether it's the stretching before a physical work-out (I'm not speaking from personal experience here!); the Pixar 'short' that precedes the main movie; the guy who comes on stage to tell a few jokes ahead of the star act – all play a part in the preparation for what's to come.

In line with the other gospels, Matthew records the coming of John the Baptist ahead of Jesus' ministry. In appearance, he's an Elijah-type figure, living a simple life in the desert, away from civilisation. Jewish tradition had the return of Elijah as an essential pre-requisite of the Messiah's arrival and the passage records how people were flocking from the towns and villages to check him out for themselves. Once there, they found that what he was preaching was more significant than what he looked like.

In those days, the roads would have been little more than compacted earth tracks, with one exception: kings would order the building of stone roads, to make their journeying both more comfortable and more impressive. When the king was due to arrive, the cry would go up for local residents to prepare the way for him. John was calling for the way to be cleared not just for the Lord but for the King.

This clearing was a heart-work rather than a practical act. John was calling the people to repentance, to turn away from their sin and their ungodly lifestyles so that their hearts might be softened ready for the ministry Jesus would do among them. Without that repentance and subsequent baptism, the refreshing waters of Jesus' love would have merely bounced off the hardened surface of their lives.

Jesus, I pray that my heart would be always yielded to you. Please show me where I need to change. Help me to forgive more readily so I can be a clean vessel for your love. Amen.

JANE WALTERS

What do you mean, 'if'?

Then the devil took him to the holy city and set him on the highest point of the temple. 'If you are the Son of God,' he said, 'throw yourself down.' (vv. 5–6, NIV)

The church I used to go to took care to prepare its baptism candidates. 'Expect to have trouble in the days before. Enjoy the day; then expect to have trouble in the days following. Satan hates it when believers get baptised.' Many of us can relate to that, I'm sure!

Jesus has just been baptised in the River Jordan by John the Baptist. As he came up from the water, heaven opened above him, releasing a dove, along with the words, 'This is my Son, whom I love; with him I am well pleased' (3:17). He seems all set, but instead of launching himself into ministry, Jesus finds himself led by the Holy Spirit into the desert. For 40 days and nights (with echoes of Moses' 40 years in the wilderness), Jesus endures loneliness, hunger, thirst and, worst of all, Satan's torments.

Though we have all experienced temptations of many forms – and with differing outcomes – it's important to understand that Jesus' messianic mission lay at the heart of this wilderness time. At his baptism, his dying to his own will, God declared Jesus to be his Son. Jewish tradition had the Messiah being the Son of God, with many signs following. These included manna appearing in the wilderness once more and the Messiah declaring from the roof of the holy place that he had dominion over the world.

Let's be clear. Jesus was indeed the Son of God – no 'if' about it! He could have easily turned stones into bread or commanded angels to catch him if he jumped; and he most certainly was Lord of all the earth. His temptation lay in the path he would walk. Would he travel as the prophesied suffering servant, or claim kingship without facing the cross? There was only one choice he could make.

Father, you've called me by name, and I am yours. Help me to remember my identity as your child so I can stand against whatever accusations or temptations the enemy throws at me. I only want to honour you. Amen.

JANE WALTERS

Jesus: the new Moses

Now when Jesus saw the crowds, he went up on a mountainside and sat down. His disciples came to him, and he began to teach them. He said: 'Blessed are the poor in spirit, for theirs is the kingdom of heaven. Blessed are those who mourn, for they will be comforted.' (vv. 1–4, NIV)

I wonder if you can remember the last sermon you heard. If you're anything like me, you might remember the great joke the preacher told at the beginning but not the points he or she went on to make afterwards. Today, we're looking at the sermon on the mount, probably the most significant delivery of Jesus' teaching and the motherlode in terms of learning what it means to live as a Christian.

There are obvious echoes of Moses here. He received the ten commandments up a mountain, meeting God within the hiding place of cloud. Back then, the giving of the law was intended to keep God's people on the straight and narrow, showing them what life's priorities should look like and pointing to God. Sadly, it didn't work out well. Throughout the Old Testament we see a perpetual cycle of turning to God, then disobeying and turning away, followed by sometimes-reluctant repentance and turning back to him. It's all too easy to live like that.

Jesus, the Messiah, has come as a new Moses, one who will rescue and deliver his people once and for all. He passes down God's wisdom to his disciples in plain sight of the crowds that flock to him. The message is no longer 'stay back because this place is holy' but 'draw near and I will make you holy'. And this new Moses is delivering a new way of seeking after God and serving him, summed up in the eight beatitudes which start this teaching. The kingdom of heaven they've been waiting for can now be theirs.

The ten commandments and the other laws demanded obedience whether your heart was in it or not. In fulfilling the law, Jesus makes clear that, from now on, our inner attitude is what counts.

Jesus, thank you for the blessings you promise when I put you first. Help me seek after you more than the things of this world, and let your kingdom come. Amen.

JANE WALTERS

The suffering servant in action

When evening came, many who were demon-possessed were brought to him, and he drove out the spirits with a word and healed all who were ill. This was to fulfil what was spoken through the prophet Isaiah: 'He took up our infirmities and bore our diseases.' (vv. 16–17, NIV)

When I was nine years old, I had to learn from memory the beginning of Isaiah 53. The prize for my recital was an umbrella: so appropriate since this scripture has proved a shield and a banner over my whole life. Matthew is quoting from one of the four Suffering Servant passages in Isaiah, which all point towards the Messiah, in order to demonstrate that Jesus is the living embodiment of those prophecies in his life and in his death on the cross – which we remember especially today, Good Friday.

The cleansing of the leper is highly significant. Leprosy was a tortuous, highly contagious condition for which there was no known cure. Containment was the only answer, resulting in sufferers being banished from society. It was a desperately lonely, ugly life. The law of Moses stipulated the sacrifices to be made when a person recovered but they were never required because no one ever did. Jesus, the Messiah, the new Moses, is doing what the law could not. I'd love to have seen the look on the priest's face when the healed leper presented himself!

The second healing in this chapter is equally groundbreaking because it concerned a Gentile. The Roman centurion is commended for showing more faith in Jesus' ability to heal his servant than all the Jews. The day is coming, Jesus goes on to declare, when the kingdom of heaven will expand into all humanity. Faith matters more than religious heritage.

Third, a healing much closer to home: his friend's mother-in-law. Healings don't have to take place on platforms or in front of crowds; nor do they have to involve life-threatening conditions. Jesus is willing to step into every situation, large or small, for those he loves. Will you let him step into yours, today?

Spend some time thinking about Jesus, the suffering servant, going to the cross for you. Let some of the enormity of that sacrifice sink in; then thank him for what he won for you: your salvation, wholeness and healing.

JANE WALTERS

The servant king – and truest friend

This was to fulfil what was spoken through the prophet Isaiah: 'Here is my servant whom I have chosen, the one I love, in whom I delight; I will put my Spirit on him, and he will proclaim justice to the nations.' (vv. 17–18, NIV)

Jesus has once more fallen foul of the religious authorities, this time about his apparent flouting of sabbath law. Not only had his disciples picked some corn but he'd also had the audacity to heal a man with a withered hand, restoring not only his health but his work-life. How dreadful! It was enough for the Pharisees to consider doing away with Jesus, so he left the region – only to be followed by crowds of needy people.

It gives the gospel author another opportunity to show how Jesus fulfils the Messianic prophecies, this time quoting (with some adaptation) Isaiah 42. Listen to how tenderly God refers to his beloved suffering servant: 'The one I love, in whom I delight.' There are reminders here of Jesus' baptism, when the voice of God breaks through from heaven, declaring, 'This is my Son, whom I love; with him I am well pleased' (3:17). These are the sentiments of a doting father, proud – if that's the right word – to call his son his own.

The attributes God ascribes to the Messiah are not positive ones, recalling what he is and does; but they are seen in the reverse: what he never is and never does. At first glance, the first, 'He will not quarrel or cry out', might read as passive, that he's not one to make a fuss. We mustn't confuse that with not making an impact! Any of us who have felt like a bruised reed, trampled on and unable to stand, or a smouldering wick, so burned out that we're barely existing, can be utterly grateful that this chosen one chooses to stoop to our level and bring healing, strength and revival, to say nothing of the justice he will one day bring to the entire global community.

Jesus, I'm in awe that your lovingkindness extends even to me. On days when I feel so broken, in such a mess, I can trust you not only to notice but also to come close to help. Thank you, Lord. Amen.

JANE WALTERS

All I need is found in Jesus

'We have here only five loaves of bread and two fish,' they answered. 'Bring them here to me,' he said… Taking the five loaves and the two fish and looking up to heaven, he gave thanks and broke the loaves. (vv. 17–19, NIV)

Part of every parent's job description is sandwich maker. The more sensible ones get their children trained in spreading as soon as they are weaned. I wasn't one of those. And as we pop all the lunch components into the pack, we know that a soft cheese triangle might get traded for someone else's grapes; that kind of sharing is all par for the course. Can you imagine, though, a parent's astonishment at hearing that their son's trading resulted in thousands upon thousands of people being fed?

Jews have long believed that when the Messiah comes, he will bring bread from heaven and, particularly, bread in the desert. (A further extension of Jesus being the new Moses, as we've previously seen.) We have both here. Thousands of hungry people, restless and irritable, are in a remote place with no provision. Then Jesus takes this humble packed meal, offers it to heaven and begins to break it and break it and break it until there is so much to share that even the amount of leftovers is overwhelming.

In John's account of this same miracle, we read that Jesus says, not long afterwards, 'I am the bread of life' (John 6:35). He is our ultimate nourishment, the only one in whom we find complete satisfaction. Yet, particularly at Eastertime, our focus is on the way Jesus gave himself up to be broken on our behalf. It's something we consciously recall in Communion when, as believers, we share the Lord's Supper, breaking the bread and drinking from the cup.

There is a further Messianic message here, too. Not only can we look back and see Jewish expectation being fulfilled but we can also look ahead to the wonderful heavenly banquet referred to in Revelation 19 as the 'wedding supper of the Lamb'.

Jesus, through your sacrifice and glorious rising again, you have provided all I ever need, now and in the future. I worship you now, laying myself down as an offering. All praise to you! Amen.

JANE WALTERS

A confession and a turning point

'But what about you?' he asked. 'Who do you say I am?' Simon Peter answered, 'You are the Messiah, the Son of the living God.'
(vv. 15–16, NIV)

You've got to love Simon Peter. Bold, brash, known for putting his foot in it – quite literally when getting out of the boat in a storm – and not afraid of saying what's on his mind. I suspect that even he was surprised at what he said on this particular day. Sometimes we don't realise what we're thinking or feeling until we say it out loud.

This passage is astonishing for several reasons. First, its context. Jesus travelled with his disciples – perhaps to get some privacy – to Caesarea Philippi, a town which had been renamed in honour of the emperor and was dominated by pagan worship. Surrounded by other gods to choose from, both human and mythological, Jesus asks, 'Do you recognise that I'm God?'

Second, Peter's intuition. Jesus has often hinted at his true identity and has given the disciples enough teaching to point clearly in the right direction, yet the others don't seem to have joined the dots to reveal the full picture. Asked the more general question, 'What do other people think?', they offer John the Baptist (a strange answer, given that Jesus and John appeared in public together), Elijah or one of the other prophets. Up until now, no one has directly declared Jesus to be the Messiah. Peter is the first, cutting through doubt and mystery and marking a turning point in Jesus' ministry – and his own life.

Third, what Simon Peter actually says. Jesus has previously referred to himself as the Son of Man and the disciples have once called him the Son of God (14:33), but this is the first time that he's been described as both Messiah and the Son of God, both titles fulfilling Old Testament prophecy.

From now on, the whole tone of Matthew's gospel is set to change.

'What about you?' Imagine that Jesus is asking you this, right here in this moment. Open your heart to him; tell him what's on your mind. Wait in the silence, then listen for his reply.

JANE WALTERS

A glimpse of the Messiah's glory

After six days Jesus took with him Peter, James and John the brother of James, and led them up a high mountain by themselves. There he was transfigured before them. His face shone like the sun, and his clothes became as white as the light. (vv. 1–2, NIV)

If you've ever been hill-walking or mountain-climbing, you'll know that the sheer slog of getting to the top is more than rewarded by the view when you get there. In today's passage, Jesus takes Peter, James and John for a hike up a high mountain, likely Mount Hermon, in order to pray. None of them would have anticipated what happens: a powerful, all-too-brief revelation of the Messiah's glory. No doubt the author's attempts to describe the sight are woefully inadequate – how can earthly words possibly describe heavenly visions? – but we get the idea.

When Moses asked God to show him his glory (Exodus 33:18), he was told to hide in a rock while God passed by. Here, Moses is present to witness this glory in God's Son, accompanied by Elijah, making his long-promised return. Both men, representing the law and the prophets, are pointing again to Jesus being the Messiah, for whom they prepared the way.

Within the cover of a bright cloud, God repeats the affirmation he made at Jesus' baptism: 'This is my Son, whom I love; with him I am well pleased' (v. 5). This title, *agapetos*, or beloved, was a familiar Jewish messianic term and serves to confirm Peter's confession of Christ that we read yesterday. It's as if God is putting his seal of endorsement on Jesus. Whether people recognise Jesus as Messiah or not, there is no doubt that God has declared him to be so.

The disciples were, understandably, in awe from everything they were witnessing. The sights, the sounds, all beyond human reckoning. When Jesus urged them back to standing, the heavenly visitors had gone – with no need for Peter's blustering hospitality after all. It was just them on the mountaintop once more. But things would never be the same again.

Jesus, thinking of your glory makes me bow in awe and adoration. Holy King, precious Lord, chosen Messiah, I worship you. Amen.

JANE WALTERS

Behold your king!

This took place to fulfil what was spoken through the prophet: 'Say to Daughter Zion, "See, your king comes to you, gentle and riding on a donkey, and on a colt, the foal of a donkey."' (vv. 4–5, NIV)

Few will forget the pageantry of the state funeral of Queen Elizabeth II in October 2022. All around the globe, people were transfixed by the scenes on their televisions, played out hour by hour. 'Utterly appropriate,' we might have concluded. 'Fit for a queen.'

Our passage today stands in stark contrast, despite it centring on the greatest king of all time. Yet it highlights what we have seen again and again in the scriptures, and experienced in our own lives, that God's kingdom operates by very different rules. Reading ahead, in Matthew 23:11–12, we can see Jesus' summary: 'The greatest among you will be your servant. For those who exalt themselves will be humbled, and those who humble themselves will be exalted' – something Jesus modelled throughout his life.

My Bible titles this passage 'The triumphal entry' and yet there is something curiously non-triumphant about it. For a start, Jesus knows that this journey will take him towards suffering and humiliation – hardly causes for celebration. And what of his mode of transport? We mustn't think that he was riding a donkey because all the war-horses were already hired out that day! In fact, it's obvious that he had planned ahead, arranging everything with the colt owner, so that Zechariah's prophecy would be fulfilled.

Matthew describes 'a very large crowd' (v. 8) coming to meet this most non-Messiah-like Messiah, throwing their cloaks for him to ride over – as they would for royalty – and cheering and crying out, 'Hosanna' (which means 'God save'). Apparently, Jesus is the talk of the whole city with people asking, 'Who is this?' It strikes me that this is one of our responsibilities as Christians: to honour the Lord Jesus and make him known in the midst of non-believers and those of different opinions.

Jesus, I worship you as Saviour and Lord, and yet so many around me don't even recognise you. Help me to bear witness to you today, for your glory. Amen.

JANE WALTERS

Every question deserves an answer

While the Pharisees were gathered together, Jesus asked them, 'What do you think about the Messiah? Whose son is he?' 'The son of David,' they replied. (v. 41, NIV)

One of the most frustrating seasons for a mother is the one where her child constantly asks, 'Why?' I've recently returned to this phase in the lives of my grandchildren and, although I have more patience these days, I still find myself trying to give answers through gritted teeth or, buying time, turning it around and asking, 'Why do you think it is?'

Jesus loved to ask questions! In fact, he is recorded in the gospels asking 307 of them. (In turn, he is asked 183 questions, of which he only directly answers three.) He's already asked his disciples who they thought he was but now he's with the Pharisees, his staunch opponents. You'll note that Jesus' question doesn't directly reference himself; rather he makes it more general as he draws them into debate.

They weren't wrong in the answer they gave. One of the chief attributes of the foretold Messiah was that he would, indeed, be from the line of David. There wasn't a rabbi who would have answered differently. But, in asking the question, Jesus was challenging them to think more deeply, explore more thoroughly. It reminds me of the time I tried to witness to a good friend of mine. She agreed with every statement I made about Jesus, but she was no nearer to him after our chat than she'd been at the beginning.

The psalm Jesus quotes from clearly points to the Messiah having heavenly attributes. True, he is David's earthly descendant, but he is so much more than that too. The sad thing is that the Pharisees and all the other gainsayers would have had all their hopes and expectations for the Messiah not only met but exceeded if they had accepted Jesus' claims. The truth only sets you free if you believe it!

Jesus, thank you that you never impose yourself on us but draw us by invitation. I pray I would hear your voice today and be open to what you ask of me. Amen.

JANE WALTERS

Life or death: the choice is yours

'What shall I do, then, with Jesus who is called the Messiah?' Pilate asked. They all answered, 'Crucify him!' (v. 22, NIV)

We have reached the darkest hours in the life of Jesus Christ, the Messiah. The hours spent confronting the religious leaders during his ministry, sometimes having to escape their murderous intent towards him, have led to this. It's the final showdown and it's not looking good.

Jesus faces two trials: one in front of the Jewish leaders and the other the Romans. Before today's verses, we can read of his encounter with Caiaphas who asks him a direct question about his identity (considered illegal in court). 'Tell us if you are the Messiah, the Son of God' (26:63). Throughout his ministry, Jesus has not himself directly said this, though there have been statements he has not denied. His answer, 'You have said so' (27:11), has led him to face the judgement of the Romans, who alone could pass down punishment.

Pilate asks the question that all of us face at some point and it's always a matter of life or death. Do we accept that Jesus is the Son of God? The one who came to save us from our sins? And if so, what do we do with that knowledge? Receive it, embrace it, find life through its truths? Or deny it, ignore it, choose to stumble on through life in the dark? For Pilate, of course, the consequences were not solely for him but for this man Jesus, who stood before him, innocent of every charge.

The detail about Pilate's wife is interesting, with God appearing in the sixth dream recorded in this gospel. Through it, she has been persuaded of Jesus' innocence and sends a message to her husband, urging him to drop the case. Perhaps the message never reached him. Perhaps Pilate was too weak-willed. The people cried, 'Crucify him!' The die was cast.

Spend a few minutes thinking about the people around you who don't know Jesus, or those who've been told but haven't yet made a decision. Pray that they would know the truth, embrace it for themselves and live for him.

JANE WALTERS

Ever present, ever Lord

'Therefore go and make disciples of all nations, baptising them in the name of the Father and of the Son and of the Holy Spirit, and teaching them to obey everything I have commanded you. And surely I am with you always, to the very end of the age.' (vv. 19–20, NIV)

We've come to the final day of our whistle-stop tour of Matthew's gospel. We've traced the evidence of Jesus' messiahship through his birth, teaching, miracles and interaction with the people around him. We've followed the author's careful pointing out of Jesus' pedigree in the fulfilling of many scriptures and have seen where it ultimately led him: the cross.

One of the first pieces of evidence for Jesus being the Messiah stemmed from being the baby born Immanuel, 'God with us'. The disciples have had this truth as their experience for three years, living and working alongside him in close community. But the crucifixion seemed to change everything. Despite Jesus' care in teaching and warning them ahead of time what was going to happen, his death left them bereft, confused and heart-stricken.

True to his word, though, he is gloriously risen. The other gospel accounts reveal that Jesus met with his disciples on several occasions, but Matthew describes only one. And what a one! Gathered once more on a mountainside, the time has come to pass his messianic authority on to them. What they experienced as a mission trip in chapter 10 is to become their way of life: sharing the good news and not just creating new converts but baptising and discipling them. There's a real sense of legacy here. The disciples, the ones who have spent these years learning, become the teachers, inspired by the greatest teacher of all time.

The gospel closes where it started: Jesus will be Immanuel, God with us for as long as the earth endures. Though many still fail to recognise him, the Messiah has indeed come, bringing in the promised kingdom of God. And, through the faithful witness of his servants, this kingdom will be extended throughout the earth. Hallelujah!

Jesus, how else can we respond but to worship you? You are glorious, Messiah, name above all names. Help us receive your great commission afresh, demonstrate your love and win the lost wherever we go. Amen.

JANE WALTERS

What does it mean to be a 'living sacrifice'?

Lyndall Bywater writes:

The book of Romans is an epic epistle! Paul probably wrote it in about AD57, during his three years in Corinth. The longest of his 13 letters in the Bible, it stretches over 16 chapters, retelling the arc of human history from God's perspective: the wonder of creation, the devastation caused by sin and the futility of humankind's best efforts to put things right; then the coming of Jesus, his life, death and resurrection, and our adoption into God's family; the work of the Spirit in helping us live out our new identity as children of God, and then the complex relationship between the Jewish people and the Gentile believers who've joined the body of Christ. And that's all in the first eleven chapters!

Chapter 12 opens with a 'therefore'. The first thing I remember learning about reading the New Testament letters was that, when you see a 'therefore', you need to ask what it's there for. In the case of 12:1, the 'therefore' is the pivot on which the whole letter turns. If all of this is true, Paul seems to be saying, then this is what it means for you.

Later in that verse, Paul uses two words which have caused much pondering to Bible scholars down the years. He says that we are to be 'living sacrifices'. It's not a phrase he used often, though towards the end of his life he did refer to himself as a drink offering being poured out (2 Timothy 4:6). Over the next two weeks, we're going to look at these two words, 'living sacrifice', and ponder what they might mean for us.

The phrase can only come alive for us if we get some idea of what it might have meant to Paul's readers, so we'll spend the first week having a look at what they would have understood by the word 'sacrifice'. That will help us grasp the difference between traditional sacrifices and living ones, then we'll spend the second week thinking about how being a living sacrifice changes the way we live our everyday lives.

I confess, I find the book of Romans a bit daunting, but I have so enjoyed writing these notes, and my hope and prayer is that you will enjoy discovering the depths of this quirky little two-word phrase as much as I have.

Just... wow!

Everything comes from him; Everything happens through him; Everything ends up in him. (v. 36, MSG)

If you're a fan of 'makeover TV', you'll be familiar with the story of a family who've reached the end of their tether, living in a house that's falling down around them. They plan a short break to get away from it all, wearied by how much work they need to do to put things right, and defeated by how much it'll cost. Little do they know, friends and family have applied to a TV show on their behalf for one of those super-fast renovations. When they get home, all they can do is stand in the middle of their beautifully decorated living room and cry, because suddenly it's all been done. All they have to do is live in it.

The apostle Paul has much weightier matters on his mind than house renovations, but what we're reading here in the cross-over from Romans 11 to Romans 12 is precisely that sort of moment. He's taken eleven chapters to explain what a mess our proverbial human house was in, how we were stuck trying to fix ourselves and exhausted because we never could. Then came Jesus, who did it all for us. He lived the perfect human life, the life we know we should live. He died the death of a criminal, soaking into himself every failure, every horror, every depravity we humans have ever committed. He was raised to life, conquering death, the one enemy we had no power against. Then he gave us the keys to our lives – rescued and transformed.

It's all been done. As we stand in the midst of total redemption, we look around in wonder. It'll take a while to discover everything we've been given, but for now all we need to do is live in it.

Jesus, everything comes from you; thank you for everything you've given me.
Jesus, everything happens through you; thank you that you're leading me.
Jesus, everything ends in you; thank you for bringing me to completion. Amen.
LYNDALL BYWATER

From death to life

Present your bodies as a living sacrifice… Simon Peter answered, 'You are the Messiah, the Son of the living God.' (Romans 12:1 and Matthew 16:16, NRSV)

I recently visited the site of Caesaria Philippi, where Peter spoke these words recorded in Matthew 16. It's beautiful and peaceful these days, with spectacular scenery, fascinating caves and beautiful water courses, but in Jesus' time it would have been a rather dark place to visit. It was a place of sacrifice where many animals, and even children, met their end. It would have had a stench of death about it.

I stood there thinking about Peter, and suddenly the word 'living' leapt out at me from his declaration. Amid all that death, he proclaimed Jesus to be 'the Son of the living God'. It's as though he caught a glimpse of the sheer 'aliveness' of Jesus in spite of all the death and darkness around him.

'Living' is the first word I want to draw your attention to in our reflections on Romans 12:1. Paul talks about sacrifices, which by their very nature are normally dead, but he calls his readers to be 'living sacrifices'. What does that mean?

Jesus stood among the death and darkness of Caesaria Philippi and gave Peter a commission; he gave him a new name and a new purpose. Elaborate acts of worship and devotion were going on around them, but it's as though Jesus was saying: 'Your act of worship needs to be to go and live the life I'm giving you.'

Has it ever occurred to you that living life to the full is one of the most precious things you can do for God? When life seems full of difficult things, painful things, trivial things and downright dull things, it's easy to get cynical and disillusioned, but our life is a gift of grace and when we live it wholeheartedly, we delight the heart of God.

Jesus, Son of the living God, renew my love for life. When boredom dulls my senses, when pain takes my breath, when hopelessness tempts me to give up, fill me with your boundless life and help me choose to live. Amen.

LYNDALL BYWATER

From debt to gift

Therefore, I urge you, brothers and sisters, in view of God's mercy, to offer your bodies as a living sacrifice, holy and pleasing to God. (v. 1, NIV)

Robert was unimpressed when his probation officer told him his 150 hours of community service would be spent gardening in the local churchyard. He'd done his best to avoid God all his life, and religious people made him angry. A year later, when his hours were done and his debt to society was paid, he asked if he could have a word with the vicar.

'I'll be back next Saturday. I used to come because I had to, but now I'm going to come because I want to.'

If you'd asked Paul's readers the main reason for making sacrifices, they'd probably have said it was to put things right with God; to pay a debt and to earn God's approval. But Paul tucks an important little phrase into this verse which turns the whole idea of sacrifice on its head. In the NIV it's translated, 'in view of God's mercy'. In Jewish and Roman religious culture, sacrifice came first, then you got the mercy once you'd paid your debt. Now, in the wonderful new kingdom of Jesus, mercy comes first. Before we've paid a single debt, we are forgiven and made right with God. What a breathtaking thought!

Two thousand years later, we don't tend to make the kind of sacrifices the Jewish and Roman religions required, but we're surprisingly good at trying to earn God's approval. All too often, we assume that the mercy will only come when we do the right things: work hard, go to church, pray more, be more patient, tell more people about Jesus. Those are all wonderful things to do, but let's remember that we already have God's love and approval before we do a single one. By all means let's do those things – not because we have to but because we want to.

Are you aware of doing certain things to win God's approval or earn his mercy? What are the things you find yourself doing more out of 'ought' than 'want'?

LYNDALL BYWATER

From perfect to present

For we are God's masterpiece. He has created us anew in Christ Jesus, so we can do the good things he planned for us long ago. (Ephesians 2:10, NLT)

The tale is told of a piano maestro who was performing a concert at a prestigious venue. Shortly before he was due to come on stage, a six-year-old boy in the audience took it upon himself to jump up on the stage, sit down at the magnificent grand piano and start playing. So engrossed was he in the sound which his tiny fingers produced that he hardly noticed the old man who stepped up behind him, put one arm either side of his little body and wrapped a complex accompaniment around his simple little tune. The maestro turned the little boy's faltering notes into beautiful music.

For the past few days, we've been considering what the word 'sacrifice' might have meant to Paul's readers, and today we come to the fact that sacrifices had to be perfect. You couldn't just bring any old animal, bird or pot of grain to give to God. It had to be without blemish and of the highest quality. Temple sellers had even made a trade out of telling people their offerings wouldn't be sufficiently perfect so they should buy something extra on their way to the temple. That's partly why Jesus got so furious that he overturned their tables (Mark 11:15–17). The idea of 'perfect' was being used to swindle people.

We don't bring sacrifices to God like that, but if we're honest, that word 'perfect' can still be a bit of an issue, particularly when it turns into perfectionism. How often do you berate yourself for making mistakes or not doing things well enough?

Paul talks about living sacrifices being pleasing to God. It's not about getting everything right; it's about bringing our living selves to God just as we are and letting God make something beautiful with our lives.

As you go about your day, try to remember that showing up and doing your best is far more precious to God than getting everything right. You could wear something to remind you that presence matters more than perfection.

LYNDALL BYWATER

From somewhere to everywhere

'Together, we are his house, built on the foundation of the apostles and the prophets. And the cornerstone is Christ Jesus himself. We are carefully joined together in him, becoming a holy temple for the Lord.' (Ephesians 2:20–21, NLT)

My Bible geography is limited, so I have never quite appreciated the journeys people would have made to get to the temple for the Jewish festivals. When I visited the Holy Land, we made that journey in a bus, starting from the River Jordan, some 400 metres below sea level, and driving the 45-minute journey up to the city of Jerusalem, some 800 metres above sea level. That's 1,200 metres of climb in just 30 kilometres of distance. And the Israelites did it on foot or riding animals! Going up to Jerusalem wasn't an optional extra. It was part of a faithful expression of worship to God, and one of the reasons for going was to make the appropriate sacrifices. Sacrifices couldn't be made anywhere. They had to be offered at the temple.

So far, we've considered how Paul was helping his readers to think differently about sacrifice in the light of Jesus. He was helping them understand that there was no longer a need to pay their debts to God or to provide a perfect offering, but Paul was also encouraging them to let go of the idea that God could only be properly worshipped in a designated place. Instead of taking sacrifices to a place which was full of God's presence, they themselves were to be living sacrifices, temples brimming over with God's presence whatever they did and wherever they went.

When we think about carrying God's presence everywhere, we often think that means telling everyone we meet about Jesus, but what if we took a broader view? Perhaps being a carrier of God's presence is also about pausing to pray wherever we go, and doing our bit to bring peace and joy, whatever we're doing.

A thought to ponder and wonder at: God would rather take up residence in you – in your life, no matter how chaotic, messy or humdrum it may seem – than live in the most spectacularly beautiful building in all the world.

LYNDALL BYWATER

From somebody to anybody

'Do not regard your servant as a worthless woman, for I have been speaking out of my great anxiety and vexation all this time.' (v. 16, NRSV)

Being a gatekeeper is powerful. You'll know this if you've ever picked up the phone to make a GP appointment, only to experience mild dread at the thought of having to justify your request to the receptionist without going into intimate details. He or she has the power to grant you access or to deny it, to favour you or to turn you away, sending you back to the even more daunting E-consult service. I exaggerate for effect, since most GP receptionists I've come across have been lovely, but you get the gist.

For the Jewish people, the priest was the gatekeeper to the presence and favour of God. If you displeased the priest, he might reject your offering or even send you away. Hannah's story is evidence that when access to God is mediated by human beings, things go wrong. The priest, Eli, decided she wasn't worthy of access to God and, had she not stood up for herself, he'd have turned her out of the temple courts altogether.

One of the staggering new ideas Paul's readers needed to grasp was the truth that they no longer needed priests to make them acceptable to God. Jesus had flung wide the door for anyone to come to God freely and without restrictions. It's a lesson we, the church, are still learning today. If anyone has ever made you feel like a 'worthless woman', if anyone has ever suggested you're not acceptable to God or made you feel like you're the wrong shape and you don't belong, they weren't doing it in Jesus' name. As far as Jesus is concerned, you don't need a 'somebody' to approve you; you can come knowing you're completely loved for who you are.

Has someone in church leadership ever spoken words to you which have made you feel misunderstood or excluded? Bring those words to God in prayer and ask the Holy Spirit to replace them with words of truth and grace.

LYNDALL BYWATER

From mine to God's

So, my brothers and sisters, you also died to the law through the body of Christ, that you might belong to another, to him who was raised from the dead, in order that we might bear fruit for God. (v. 4, NIV)

I've lived in several different homes during my adult life, all of which I've owned or part-owned. When it's been time to move on, I've been fortunate enough to be able to keep them and let them out, usually to people I know. It's a real blessing to do that, but it does have one down-side, namely that I get to go back to these homes I've lovingly made my own, only to find the tenants have changed everything! It certainly tests my ability to let go.

We've been thinking about sacrifices this week, and there's no doubt that bringing a sacrifice was an all-or-nothing business. You couldn't bring an offering and then ask the priest if you could have some of it back to take home. When you made your sacrifice, you gave it up completely. It wasn't yours anymore; it belonged to God.

Now we're the sacrifices – living, loving, rejoicing in our freedom to come to God as we are, but sacrifices, nonetheless. We don't have to be perfect, or find a priest or temple to go to, but we do have to give ourselves irrevocably to God if we want to live the abundant life Jesus offers.

But this isn't the sombre, demeaning kind of self-giving; this is a joyful pledging of ourselves to the only one who has ever truly been worthy of us. Maybe that's why Paul uses marriage imagery to describe this 'belonging' to God. Marriage is a sacrifice of sorts. It's giving ourselves completely to another, to enter a life of joyful union.

That's what God invites us to. The sacrificing is real. We let go; we give ourselves completely to God. But the joyful union is also real, and worth every bit of the sacrifice.

Do you have some jewellery you could wear today as a reminder to stop every so often and enjoy the truth that you belong to God, not as an object or a chattel but as a beloved bride?

LYNDALL BYWATER

Bringing our bodies

As she stood behind him at his feet weeping, she began to wet his feet with her tears. Then she wiped them with her hair, kissed them and poured perfume on them. (v. 38, NIV)

Had she come to make things right? Had she come to plead mercy for the destructive lifestyle she'd got stuck in? Had she prepared a speech or brought something that might make atonement for her soul? As she stood waiting for an opportunity to speak to Jesus discreetly, her body got ahead of her. Before she knew it, she was crying, great gulping sobs of sorrow and penitence. She was getting his feet all wet, so she tried drying them with her hair. And then, in that tornado of emotions, suddenly she was kissing those precious feet.

When I read Romans 12:1, the word I find most difficult is 'bodies'. Paul says we are to bring our bodies to be living sacrifices. I'd far rather bring my rational mind or even my very full heart than my body. Perhaps I'm just the product of centuries of Christianity which has tended to think that things that come out of our heads (like words, ideas, beliefs and reasonings) are more important and more acceptable to God than things we do with our physical bodies. Perhaps it's the physicality of this story that makes it so shocking. We imagine Jesus awkwardly putting up with the ministrations of a rather tactile woman, like the 'non-huggy' person at church who stands stiffly through a series of unwelcome embraces, but that's not what happens. He takes pleasure in her affection. Her body is as acceptable to him as is her mind and heart.

Whether you love it or hate it, whether you're forever trying to improve it or you've given up on it altogether, your body is beautiful. Bring God all the offerings you like – wheat-sheafs, turtledoves, incense or a collection plate of cash – but he would choose your body anytime.

How do you feel when you reflect on the fact that God loves your body as much as your heart, mind and soul? What might you do today to treat your body well?

LYNDALL BYWATER

A restoration transformation

Do not conform to the pattern of this world, but be transformed by the renewing of your mind. (v. 2, NIV)

The Repair Shop is one of the most popular makeover TV programmes of recent years. Its simple format has proved to be compelling viewing for millions of people, and King Charles III has even availed himself of its services. People bring their much-loved possessions – objects which have been damaged, either through incident, accident or the rigours of time – and the talented team of experts get to work, lovingly restoring each piece to its former glory.

Having looked at what sacrifices meant to the Jewish people and how we might understand ourselves as living sacrifices, we turn our attention to verse two of Romans 12, to consider what it might mean to live out this unusual calling. We first discover that it's going to involve transformation. Paul's readers had to change not only the way they saw sacrifices, but also their way of seeing everything. There was a 'pattern' which the world around them followed – a pattern which informed everything they thought and did – but the new Christian community was to ditch that pattern completely. They were to let the Spirit of God renew their minds so that they would think and act differently to those around them.

This is where it helps to think about *The Repair Shop* rather than an episode of *Star Trek*. Having our minds renewed isn't about having our brains wiped so we lose our identity and come back reprogrammed. It's more like inviting the master craftsman to come and restore our fragile minds to what they were always meant to be. You were created whole and wholly good. As you entrust yourself to God, the Spirit peels back the layers of wrong thinking which have stuck to you, revealing the wonderful, loving, confident person you really are in Christ.

Lord, you created me and everything you create is good, but I've picked up some wrong habits along the way – wrong ways of seeing myself and the world. Would you clean away the grime and renew my mind? Amen.

LYNDALL BYWATER

From alone to together

We are many parts of one body, and we all belong to each other. In his grace, God has given us different gifts for doing certain things well. (vv. 5–6, NLT)

I recently visited the ancient city of Petra which is carved out of the rose-coloured stone of Jordan's desert landscape and was one of the Seven Wonders of the World. I'd been with my husband about 16 years ago, but this visit was far more enjoyable. I mean no offence to Phil, who's a great travel companion, but this time I went with a group. Being blind, I only ever really 'see' places through other people's eyes, and I felt like I experienced it so much more fully this time, in the company of 20 or 30 people who were all marvelling at its beauty. I was reminded yet again of how much richer life is when we allow ourselves to need each other.

Paul has invited his readers to offer their bodies as 'living sacrifices' and to be transformed by the renewing of their minds. Now he gives the rest of his letter over to outlining what that transformation might look like in real-life situations. He helps them see the difference between the world's patterns and the patterns of God's kingdom. The first topic he turns to is community.

We humans have a tendency to go it alone, and that's an aspect of human nature that hasn't changed much in the past 2,000 years. We prize our independence; we'd rather do things our own way than fit into a group. We might even fall into thinking we're better than everyone else. But that's world-patterned thinking. Kingdom-patterned thinking is when we recognise that we need other people, and they need us. It's enjoying being good at things but never thinking so highly of ourselves that we put others down. Being a living sacrifice means letting our lives be woven in with other people's.

Do you know your gifts or do you struggle to believe you have any? Is there an area of life where you tend to be a bit proud? Ask God to help you get your strengths and weaknesses into perspective.

LYNDALL BYWATER

From payback to peace

Do all that you can to live in peace with everyone. Dear friends, never take revenge. Leave that to the righteous anger of God. (vv. 18–19, NLT)

I love a good bit of historical fiction, rollicking tales of knights and damsels, castles and skirmishes! But there's one aspect of those tales I always find disturbing, and that's the honour code: the way every wrong has to be repaid; every slight against person or property has to be avenged, often leading to centuries of pain and unforgiveness.

In my world, I only encounter this code in stories, but this was the culture Paul's readers knew all too well, and that makes today's reading absolutely radical. They would have been steeped in a payback mindset. It's even in the Hebrew scriptures, after all: 'an eye for an eye, a tooth for a tooth' (Leviticus 24:19–20). They would have been taught that to refuse to avenge an insult or a crime was weakness, that strong, upright people give as good as they get, and yet here, Paul is telling them to leave the payback to God. That really would require a renewing of their minds.

Nowadays we have legal systems and law courts to work justice for us, but the human heart still has a knack for harbouring grudges. We may not use violence to get our due, but we're not above punishing people in other ways. Have you ever been hurt by someone, chosen to forgive them, but carried on being a bit less friendly towards them for a while, just so they know you're not amused? Don't get me wrong, being honest and telling people when they've caused us pain is important, but kingdom-pattern living means letting go of our grudges, renouncing our right to revenge and trusting that God will work justice.

It's not easy. It may take days, weeks, months, even years. But there is joy and freedom in discovering that we don't have to keep score anymore.

Is there someone you've been trying to punish? It might help to picture yourself walking with them into the presence of God, handing them over to the one who judges all things, and walking away, leaving them in God's hands.

LYNDALL BYWATER

From cynicism to honour

Be a good citizen. All governments are under God. Insofar as there is peace and order, it's God's order. So live responsibly as a citizen. (v. 1, MSG)

Being a member of Parliament isn't for the faint-hearted. In an article for *The Independent* in October 2021, one of Yvette Cooper's former advisors said that the MP had routinely received up to 50 death threats a week. The murders of Jo Cox and Sir David Amess suggest things aren't getting any better. Perhaps the saddest thing is that those who make such threats don't seem to think of their targets as humans trying to do their best in life; all they see is the office they hold or the party they stand for. Maybe that's because it's easier to hate a system or an institution than a person.

I find the first part of today's passage an uncomfortable read. I can think of many situations around the world where the authorities do not seem to be acting for the good of their people – where oppression and corruption seem to be the default leadership styles – and I do not believe God is in favour of that. So I'm heartened to find, on researching, that Paul has something different in mind. It seems more likely from the context that he was talking about synagogue authority rather than secular authority. He absolutely believed that the gospel was for the Gentiles as well as the Jewish people, but he wanted both groups to be one family of faith, and he longed for that whole family to respect the Jewish religious authorities and to pay the temple tax.

Most importantly, this passage is sandwiched between two repetitions of the command to love everyone and to love well. Integrity calls us to speak up when we believe our leaders are in error, but honouring them to the best of our ability is part of the business of loving; treating them with respect, believing the best about them and praying for them, even if we disagree with their values or their party allegiance.

Which politician frustrates you most at the moment? Spend some time today praying for them, laying aside everything you've heard about them in the media and asking the Spirit to show you how God sees them.

LYNDALL BYWATER

From judging to accepting

Blessed are those who don't feel guilty for doing something they have decided is right. But if you have doubts about whether or not you should eat something, you are sinning if you go ahead and do it. For you are not following your convictions. (vv. 22–23, NLT)

It wasn't until I lived in a small, three-bedroom flat with seven other women from five different countries that I was struck by the reality of cultural diversity. Who knew most other European cultures take their shoes off indoors and find it shocking that so many of us Brits don't; and who knew that the French find a bowl of lettuce with vinaigrette to be a perfectly acceptable starter. So many ways of doing things!

In this chapter of his letter to the Romans, Paul continues to demonstrate what it means to have a mind that doesn't conform to the patterns of this world but allows itself to be transformed and renewed. He's writing to people who were used to obeying rules as part of their religious observance, whether as Jewish or pagan worshippers. We humans always gravitate to codes and regulations. We like to know the right way to do things and we like to make sure other people are getting things right too. But suddenly Paul is saying everyone's right, even when they stick to different rules. How on earth does that work?

Kingdom-pattern living means having the Holy Spirit living in us, tuning our conscience to God's ways. Though we study the Bible and listen to godly teaching, the core of our faith is that personal connection with God in the inner room of our hearts (Matthew 6:5–6), and it's there that we shape the godly life we want to live. Isn't that dangerous? Can we be trusted? What if we get it wrong? Christianity is not a rules-based code. There isn't a set of instructions you can keep to make sure you're doing it right. It's a living, loving, growing relationship with God, and it looks different in every person who lives it.

Is there someone you know who's living out their Christian faith in a way which seems wrong to you? Try 'zooming out' from the issue you disagree with and ponder what you could learn from their relationship with God.

LYNDALL BYWATER

From observing to living

Then you will be able to test and approve what God's will is – his good, pleasing and perfect will... I myself am convinced, my brothers and sisters, that you yourselves are full of goodness, filled with knowledge and competent to instruct one another. (Romans 12:2 and 15:14, NIV)

I've been blind all my life and I've just taken up tennis. We play with audible balls – balls that rattle as they move through the air – and I'm not very good but I love it! I have friends who've played for a while and they tried to explain it to me, but it's only as I've started playing myself that I understand how it works and I'm discovering the joy of it.

Maybe that's how it is with being a living sacrifice too. When Paul's readers worshipped through dead sacrifices, there were rituals and rules to tell them exactly what to do and when: offer the right thing and your sins would be forgiven; come to the temple at the right time and you would find favour with God; engage the services of a priest and you could secure divine help for your next endeavour. But now the era of dead sacrifices is over. Now we're living sacrifices, coming just as we are, bringing ourselves, our very bodies, knowing that Jesus has done everything to restore us to relationship with God, and now we get to work out our faith by living it. Filled with God's Spirit, we feel our way, trying things out, doing our best, falling, getting up again and growing in the process. We get to work out our faith with others, building friendships, seeking counsel, helping others, journeying in community and learning to love. It's rarely tidy and it's often bewildering, but what else do you expect when you're having your mind renewed?

And we're 'full of goodness'. How amazing is that! Little old you and little old me can live lives that bring joy to God's heart and bring love to the world. That's what it means to be a living sacrifice. Who's in?

'The God of peace will soon crush Satan under your feet. The grace of our Lord Jesus be with you' (Romans 16:20, the very last verse of Paul's letter).

LYNDALL BYWATER

Our favourite characters

Jackie Harris writes:

Who is your favourite Bible character? That's the question I put to our contributors as we prepared these studies. I wonder who you would choose.

Many books of the Bible are character-driven. We might think of Ruth or Esther, the stories of Abraham, Jacob, Isaac and Joseph in Genesis or the many twists and turns in the story of David which runs through 1 and 2 Samuel, 1 Chronicles and the first two chapters of 1 Kings.

We meet many interesting characters in the pages of the Bible – some are out-and-out villains, but others are more complex. Over the next few days, our contributors will be sharing their favourites. We've generally chosen people we admire, but it is comforting to know that many of them had less-than-admirable moments in their lives. They were fallible people just like us and yet God worked with and through them.

Some of the people we have chosen are key characters and so we are just giving a snapshot or meeting them at a particular moment in their lives. Others play a more supportive role, and we may only have a small amount of information about them. We witness some characters who faced huge challenges, some whose lives were dramatically changed, some who showed great courage and others who give us an example of what not to do.

Though these men and women are distanced from us in terms of time and culture, they have much to teach us about godly living and can help us when we miss the mark. As we study their lives and experiences, we can see how they responded to the challenges they faced, how God was able to use them and how they played their part in God's plan. In doing so, we learn what we should or shouldn't do as a believer and how God might work in our individual situations. May we be encouraged as we study these individuals and learn from their stories.

Father, please speak to us through the experiences of your people. May we be inspired to see you working in our lives as you did in theirs, challenged by their example and spurred on in our own journey of faith. Amen.

Moses: a radiant but reluctant leader

Then Moses said to him, 'If your Presence does not go with us, do not send us up from here'… And the Lord said to Moses, 'I will do the very thing you have asked, because I am pleased with you and I know you by name.' (v. 15 and v. 17, NIV)

Curious, self-doubting, reluctant leader, friend of God, bargainer, negotiator, advocate, spurner of the high life, passionate, radiant with God's glory – there are so many reasons why Moses is my favourite Bible character.

I could pick so many scenes from his life to explain why but space here limits me to two. First, Exodus 3, with its sense of heaven in the ordinary, of God invading the mundane world of a shepherd and speaking directly with him. Moses' curiosity gets the better of him, he has to 'go over and see' (3:3), removing his dead animal leather shoes – inappropriate in the overwhelming presence of the living God.

When God calls him to lead his people out of slavery, Moses reacts exactly as I would have done: 'Who am I to do this? Surely, there's someone better!' Even when God promises to be with him, still Moses wheedles, 'Suppose I go… and they ask me…?' I don't know about you, but I'm so like this, imagining every possible scenario, completely forgetting how God always equips and resources us for the things he calls us to.

Later, we find Moses at Horeb (chapter 33), having led his people in a miraculous exodus from Egypt after all! He has facilitated the making of a groundbreaking covenant between God and his people. God is now telling him to move the people on. Again, we hear Moses bargaining with God, requesting a coleader and refusing to move on unless God promises to go with them, while also saying, 'Teach me your ways so I may know you' (33:13). He wants to learn God's heart, to know him. It's a powerful lesson in honesty before God and a real encounter with him.

I love that Moses implores to see God's glory here (33:18) and yet, time and again, we read of God's radiance so bright in his face that he must be veiled. I'd love to reflect God's presence like that!

HELEN WILLIAMS

Joshua: an actual superhero

'Be strong and courageous, for you are the one who will lead these people to possess all the land I swore to their ancestors I would give them. Be strong and very courageous. Be careful to obey all the instructions Moses gave you… For the Lord your God is with you wherever you go.' (vv. 6–7 and v. 9, NLT)

Imagine the scene: a fearsome army, complete with trumpets, marching around a walled city every day, for six days. Sunlight bouncing off metal. Dust clouds swirling from tramping feet. Menace permeating the walls. Shouted orders ricocheting among the stone. Then came day seven. The battle for Jericho was a key victory for the Israelites, achieved in an unprecedented manner, dependent on utter obedience to God's unusual commands. Led by Joshua.

Why do I love Joshua? He trusted God and acted on that trust. He led the nomadic Israelites into the promised land, winning battle after battle, and settled them there. He had one slip-up (a bad deal with the Gibeonites in Joshua 9). The rest of the time, he took God at his word and went for it.

I find this extraordinary. God's ways are not necessarily easy. Some days I do pretty well at putting first the kingdom of God (Matthew 6:33). I pray, delve into my Bible and commit my day, worries, thoughts and plans to my Father. I ask for his Holy Spirit to fill me. I chat to him along the way. But other days, I fail to do all these things. Not so for Joshua. He was consistent, faithful, persistent, trusting and, yes, courageous. Consequently, he experienced some of the most extraordinary events in Israel's history. He saw God at work. He went from assistant commander to leader of Israel. He formed an enduring nation from a raggle-taggle bunch of tribes.

I would love to have dinner with him and ask him how he did it. Did he ever wake up in the night in a sweat of worry? He faced rebellion, numerous attacks from foreign nations and a startling lack of trust from his fellow countrymen. But he still kept doing what God said.

Read Joshua 24:15. Joshua based his life on that initial commission from God. He was strong and courageous throughout his life. What words of God do you build your life on?

DI ARCHER

Caleb: faithful despite disappointment

'So here I am today, eighty-five years old! I am still as strong today as the day Moses sent me out; I'm just as vigorous to go out to battle now as I was then.' (vv. 10–11, NIV)

Caleb is surely one of the heroes of the Bible. He was one of the twelve scouts sent out by Moses to explore the land of Canaan and came back with an encouraging report. Unfortunately, some of the other men who had explored the land with him frightened the people with tales of giants and insurmountable problems. The result was a near revolt against Moses as the people panicked and plotted to return to Egypt. Caleb tried his best to encourage the people to trust in God's promises and to take the land, but to no avail. Because of their disobedience, everyone had to spend another 45 years wandering in the desert (Numbers 13:1—14:9).

What a disappointment that must have been, to be so close to seeing God's promise fulfilled and, through no fault of his own, face a different future. It could have made Caleb bitter and resentful, or left him disillusioned, just going through the motions as they continued in the desert. And yet, in our reading today, we see that Caleb's faith has not wavered. God had promised him that he would enter the promised land (Numbers 14:24) and he is as enthusiastic as ever to play his part in God's plan.

Caleb's courage and faithfulness challenge me. He wasn't put off by the apparent obstacles in the way. He didn't expect an easy ride but trusted that God would enable them to succeed. And he didn't let disappointment get in the way. Nor was age an issue – Caleb was still looking for adventure and new challenges, and his faith in God still burned bright.

Constancy is perhaps an old-fashioned word, but that's the quality I see in Caleb, and his example inspires me when I feel disappointed or challenged by circumstances. I hope his story will encourage you too.

Father, thank you for your constant faithfulness to me. Help me to grow in faithfulness to you and to keep my faith burning bright, even through challenging circumstances. Amen.

JACKIE HARRIS

Deborah: the superwoman

Now Deborah, a prophet, the wife of Lappidoth, was leading Israel at that time. She held court under the Palm of Deborah between Ramah and Bethel in the hill country of Ephraim, and the Israelites went up to her to have their disputes decided. (vv. 4–5, NIV)

Every year, the BBC releases its list of 100 inspiring and influential women from across the globe. The latest offering includes singer Billie Eilish, Ghanaian author Nana Darkoa Sekyiamah and Ukraine's First Lady Olena Zelenska, as well as protestors standing for change in Iran.

This year, the BBC 100 Women included the voices of several women who find themselves at the heart of conflict and war, including in Ukraine and Russia. Ten of the 100 women chosen were from Iran, with women there playing an active part in the resistance following the death of Mahsa Amini after her detention by morality police.

So often, wars around the world see women harmed through sexual violence, displacement and torture, with women often used as weapons of war. Rarely do we hear of women at the forefront of the battles. Deborah is one of five women described as a prophet in the Old Testament. She also has great wisdom, presiding over judicial matters and disputes, and is the only woman in the Bible described as a military leader, leading Israel to victory in battle. Although the translations are unclear, they indicate that Deborah was a wife and a mother – although some say the words used for these denote being a woman and a protector. Regardless, Deborah is what we might call a superwoman. Society tells us that is what we ought to be, too. To be a woman is to juggle a number of different hats constantly, to make it look easy – and of course, never to drop them. What is most important in the account of Deborah, however, is her listening to, hearing and acting on what God says. Perhaps this is what we as ordinary women – sometimes called to do extraordinary things – need to hold on to today.

God who calls us, help us to hear your voice amid the hustle and bustle of our daily lives, all the hats we wear and the titles we hold. Help us to be attuned to your voice as we navigate what it is you have called us into today. Amen.

CHINE MCDONALD

Ruth: from gloom to glory

But Ruth said: 'Entreat me not to leave you, Or *to* turn back from following after you; For wherever you go, I will go; And wherever you lodge, I will lodge; Your people *shall be* my people, And your God, my God.' (v. 16, NKJV)

Ruth is my namesake and my favourite character in the Bible. Her story is about a woman of small beginnings, who climbs to great heights. Ruth comes from a family line with a rather unpalatable beginning: an incestuous liaison (Genesis 19:30–37). Moab grew into an idolatrous nation, and it is in this context that Ruth married into an Israelite family who believed in one God, rather than *many* gods.

What prompted Ruth to follow an ageing Naomi to a land she did not know? To make 'your God, my God' (1:16)? I believe Ruth chose to follow her mother-in-law Naomi, not only out of loyalty to her, but also because she knew there must be something better than what Moab and its pagan traditions had to offer. Naomi's example, although at times punctuated by despair, showed Ruth something of the love and glory of God.

Ruth had been through grief: her husband and her brother-in-law had died in seemingly quick succession. Yet she chooses life as a widowed immigrant in Israel rather than staying in the familiar Moab. She is determined and she is courageous.

Naomi repays her daughter-in-law for her diligent care by seeking Ruth's security. Boaz is kind and financially secure; what is more, Jewish custom lays down the case for Boaz becoming Ruth's husband. Perhaps Ruth herself dreamed of one day being Boaz' wife, but it is Naomi's advice which prompts her to make her bold move on the threshing floor. Ruth's love for Naomi is special: so much so that she is described as 'being better to [Naomi] than seven sons' (4:15).

Ruth's loyal love for Naomi, and her willingness to follow the living God, result in Ruth becoming one of the ancestors of the Messiah!

How wonderfully God overwrites the pain of our lives, if only we are willing to be used by him, right where we are! What pain do you desire God to replace with his joy today? He can do it!

RUTH AKINRADEWO

Elisha: a special kind of seeing

Then Elisha prayed, 'O Lord, open his eyes and let him see!' The Lord opened the young man's eyes, and when he looked up, he saw that the hillside around Elisha was full of horses and chariots of fire. (v. 17, NLT)

The best thing about being blind is being able to navigate in the dark. It's always struck me as bonkers that airlines won't let me sit in the emergency exit row. After all, when all the lights go out, I'll be the only one who has no problem finding the door handle to open the exit.

Elisha was a man who could navigate in the dark. Maybe that's why he's always been one of my favourite Bible characters. The stories we have of him don't involve literal darkness, but they do involve situations which must have felt very dark to those who were living them: a man carrying the death-sentence of leprosy; a widow and her sons with insurmountable debts; and a city besieged by an angry king, to name but a few.

Each time, Elisha can see something no one else can. Yes, he can see a solution, but it's as though he can look deeper than that, right to the core of the person, and there he can see the root of their problem. He sees Naaman's pride and has him dip in the smelliest river around, to cleanse his leprosy. He sees the widow's loneliness, so he gets her to invite all the neighbours round, bringing their oil jars. And he sees his servant's terror, that morning in the besieged city, so he prays that his servant's fear-blindness will be lifted, and suddenly the man sees what Elisha himself has already seen: that God has everything in hand.

What Elisha teaches me is that, if we ask for spiritual sight, we can learn to look beneath the surface, beyond the obvious, even into the super-natural realm. We can see what's really going on, and we can help others to find healing and freedom.

Open my eyes, Lord. When I take things at face value, help me look again; when I get distracted by outward appearances, help me to see what really matters. Amen.

LYNDALL BYWATER

Daniel: an encouragement to persevere

'There is no other God who can deliver like this'. (v. 29, NKJV)

There are some characters in the Bible we turn to for hope and guidance and there are others who seem to seek us out.

Daniel's story is one that feels like a refrain in my life, sitting quietly (I have to confess) in the background until all of a sudden there'll be a sermon or a reading reminding me of how relevant he was to me in the past and how his experience is important to me again in that present moment.

The story of Daniel was always a favourite because it was so vivid and dramatic, but the first time his life seemed to be speaking to me particularly was when I was preparing to go to university and deciding to be a vegetarian. There was Daniel keeping to his meat-free diet. It seemed so modern and relevant.

Then I decided on a career in journalism. As a new Christian, I had a few advisers telling me it was a dangerous path, but passages from Daniel spoke to me when I gained my first proper job in media. Standing firm as a Christian in a competitive and strident environment was challenging but the message from Daniel was to stay true and be encouraged.

Much later, when a relationship failed, a job came to an end and I had to move house, life was tough. It had taken a different direction from all I'd hoped for. I was reminded again of Daniel – this time in the lions' den. Instead, then, of being broken by the circumstances, I looked to see what God would do next.

For his wisdom and faithfulness, for remaining strong in an alien environment, for giving God the glory and for remaining true to his faith and purpose even when life didn't go the way he anticipated, Daniel has been a huge source of encouragement. The prompts from his life to mine remind me time and again of the love of God.

Lord, thank you for the ways in which you remind me of your faithfulness, for speaking to me in my times of need and showing me you care about me, just as you did for Daniel. Amen.

CATHERINE LARNER

Jonah: no hiding from God

The word of the Lord came to Jonah son of Amittai: 'Go to the great city of Nineveh and preach against it, because its wickedness has come up before me.' But Jonah ran away from the Lord and headed for Tarshish. (vv. 1–3, NIV)

Mention the name Jonah and most people who have been to Sunday school would immediately think 'the whale guy'. But as with any typecast character, there's always more to them than you realise.

A little background may be helpful. Jonah lived about four miles north of Nazareth during the reign of Israel's king, Jeroboam II (793–753 BC). Five hundred miles to the east was the enemy territory of Assyria, which God planned to use to punish his wayward people, Israel. Patriotic Israelites would have prayed for Assyria's destruction, yet God told Jonah to travel to its capital city, Nineveh, to preach a message of repentance and hope.

Can you imagine the conflict raging inside him? What God was calling him to do made no sense. All the prophets before Jonah's time had been sent only to God's own people and now he was supposed to go to his enemies? Confused, he ran in the opposite direction.

As we all find out when we try it, there is no running away from God! Although the sailors threw him overboard to be drowned, God rescued him in that fabled big fish. In those disgusting bowels, Jonah finally gave in and received his second chance – not that it went well, in his opinion, when he did as he'd been commanded. Those pesky enemies went and repented, just as he'd feared! Instead of rejoicing in God's victory, Jonah was left sulking and resentful.

So, what can we learn from the story of our brother Jonah?

- God knows best, no matter how pressing our counter-argument.
- His anointing on us doesn't come off in seawater, disobedience, fear or cowardice.
- His love and mercy extend to our enemies, whether we like it or not.
- God is the God of second chances.

Lord, there are times I've run from your call and from your love. Thank you for rescuing me. Help me see the people around me through your eyes and extend to them the mercy you've shown me, with a willing heart. Amen.

JANE WALTERS

Peter: a changed person

'It is by the name of Jesus Christ of Nazareth, whom you crucified but whom God raised from the dead, that this man stands before you healed... Salvation is found in no one else, for there is no other name under heaven given to mankind by which we must be saved.' (v. 10 and v. 12, NIV)

We see Peter in the gospels as a larger-than-life character. He was a born leader, but during his three years with Jesus his impetuosity often made him ready to speak (or act) first and think second. We find him the first among the disciples to affirm Jesus as the Messiah (Matthew 16:13–20), but minutes later roundly rebuked for contradicting Jesus' warning that the religious leaders would kill him. At the last supper, Peter asserted that he would never let Jesus down, and when Jesus was arrested in Gethsemane, he pulled out his sword to cut off the ear of the high priest's servant. He risked joining the temple guard and servants round the fire, wanting to learn what was happening in Jesus' trial, hoping to remain anonymous. But his Galilean accent gave him away, and he crumpled. We know well that three times he denied having anything to do with Jesus. It is easy to say, 'What cowardice!' Then I ask myself what I would have done in that situation. I doubt if I would even have been there.

What a transformation we see in Peter after the Holy Spirit blew in only a few weeks later! After he and John were used by God to heal a man born lame, an amazed crowd gathered. Peter preached to them about Jesus; he did not mince his words. He and John were imprisoned overnight, then brought to the religious leaders and questioned about the healing. They were fearless in their reply. 'He was healed through the power of Jesus. Salvation is found in no one else.' Told – rather lamely – by the leaders to keep quiet, the supposedly ignorant Peter and John replied, 'We can't keep quiet about him.' There is more excitement to be found throughout Acts as we see Peter growing in wise leadership.

The Spirit who changed Peter wants to make you as bold for Jesus as Peter became. How might you ask God to change you? Are you willing to risk praying, 'Whatever you want to do, God, I'll let you take control'?

ROSEMARY GREEN

Lydia: an independent woman

A certain woman named Lydia, a worshipper of God, was listening to us; she was from the city of Thyatira and a dealer in purple cloth. The Lord opened her heart to listen eagerly to what was said by Paul. (v. 14, NRSV)

Lydia is the first named European Christian – a woman! Lydia follows in the footsteps of the women who were the first to see Jesus after the resurrection. Women without whom we'd have a very different Christianity – if we had a Christianity at all.

Imagine being in Lydia's shoes. It's a normal sabbath and you've gone to the place of prayer. You're accustomed to gathering there with the women of the city. You all listen curiously to these newly arrived men, Paul and Silas. Something about what they say strikes you as true. You lead your household into baptism, offering your home to these itinerant preachers.

Lydia's home was the first place European Christians met. Lydia might not be her actual name – it might merely mean 'from Lydia,' the country in Asia Minor renowned for the dyeing industry. Given how many biblical women remain completely nameless, though, I'm happy that we know that much about her. I'd got so used to hearing only about significant men in the Bible that when I realised how important Lydia was, I was really excited.

I like Lydia because she's independent. She's known because of her job, not because of her marital or parental status. Purple cloth was expensive, so it's assumed she was wealthy – able to afford a home and to offer hospitality to Paul, Silas and the other brothers and sisters. I also reflect on how Lydia models the kind of real-world life most of us lead. Hers wasn't a dramatic leaving behind of everything like the first disciples. After all, most of us stay in our jobs, and not all of us work in a church or religious organisation. God used Lydia where she was and how she was – and hers was no small role in creating the foundations of the church.

Thank you, God, for Lydia, for her willingness to listen, to lead and to create space for your church to grow. Thank you that you use our lives where we are and how we are. Amen.

SARA BATTS-NEALE

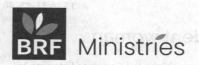

BRF Ministries

Inspiring people of all ages to grow in Christian faith

BRF Ministries is the home of Anna Chaplaincy, Living Faith, Messy Church and Parenting for Faith

As a charity, our work would not be possible without fundraising and gifts in wills.
To find out more and to donate, visit brf.org.uk/give or call +44 (0)1235 462305

Registered with
FUNDRAISING
REGULATOR

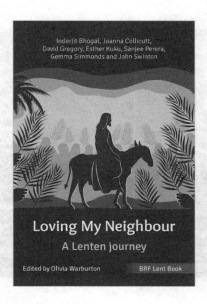

Loving My Neighbour takes us on a journey through the challenging terrain of how we can truly love one another, individually and in our communities. Daily Bible readings and reflections from Ash Wednesday to Easter Day explore how we can love in truth, love the vulnerable and the suffering, embrace difference, care for our world, and love ourselves as God loves us. Holy Week brings us back to reflect on Christ on the cross, who loved us to the very end.

Loving My Neighbour
A Lenten journey
Edited by Olivia Warburton
978 1 80039 215 1 £9.99
brfonline.org.uk

Holding Onto Hope

40 days of God's encouragement through art and reflections

Amy Boucher Pye and Leo Boucher

A 40-day journey exploring the themes of hope and new life through vivid biblical images, *Holding Onto Hope* can be used through Lent or during any 40-day period. We start with how all creation praises God and then explore the agricultural pattern of sowing, growing and harvesting before moving to the gracious promises and invitations God makes to his people. Next come images of God as our help and refuge. Finally, we focus on our new life in Christ.

Holding Onto Hope
40 days of God's encouragement through art and reflections
Amy Boucher Pye and Leo Boucher

978 1 80039 200 7 £12.99
brfonline.org.uk

To order

Online: brfonline.org.uk
Telephone: +44 (0)1865 319700
Mon–Fri 9.30–17.00

Delivery times within the UK are
normally 15 working days. Prices are
correct at the time of going to press
but may change without prior notice.

Title	Price	Qty	Total
Loving My Neighbour	£9.99		
Holding Onto Hope	£12.99		
Day by Day with God (Jan–Apr 2024) – single copy	£4.95		
Day by Day with God (May–Aug 2024) – single copy	£4.95		

POSTAGE AND PACKING CHARGES			
Order value	UK	Europe	Rest of world
Under £7.00	£2.00	Available on request	Available on request
£7.00–£29.99	£3.00		
£30.00 and over	FREE		

Total value of books	
Donation	
Postage and packing	
Total for this order	

Please complete in BLOCK CAPITALS

Title _____ First name/initials _____ Surname _____

Address _____

_____ Postcode _____

Acc. No. _____ Telephone _____

Email _____

Method of payment

❏ Cheque (made payable to BRF) ❏ MasterCard / Visa

Card no. ☐☐☐☐ ☐☐☐☐ ☐☐☐☐ ☐☐☐☐ ☐☐☐☐ ☐☐☐☐

Expires end ☐☐ M M ☐☐ Y Y Security code ☐☐☐ Last 3 digits on the reverse of the card

We will use your personal data to process this order.
From time to time we may send you information about
the work of BRF Ministries. Please contact us if you wish to discuss
your mailing preferences **brf.org.uk/privacy**

Please return this form to:

BRF Ministries, 15 The Chambers, Vineyard, Abingdon OX14 3FE | **enquiries@brf.org.uk**

For terms and cancellation information, please visit **brfonline.org.uk/terms**.

Each issue of *Day by Day with God* is available from Christian bookshops everywhere. Copies may also be available through your church book agent or from the person who distributes Bible reading notes in your church.

Alternatively, you may obtain *Day by Day with God* on subscription direct from the publishers. There are two kinds of subscription:

Individual subscriptions
covering 3 issues for 4 copies or less, payable in advance
(including postage & packing).

To order, please complete the details on page 144 and return with the appropriate payment to: BRF Ministries, 15 The Chambers, Vineyard, Abingdon OX14 3FE

You can also use the form on page 144 to order a gift subscription for a friend.

Group subscriptions
covering 3 issues for 5 copies or more, sent to one UK address (post free).

Please note that the annual billing period for group subscriptions runs from 1 May to 30 April.

To order, please complete the details on page 143 and return with the appropriate payment to: BRF Ministries, 15 The Chambers, Vineyard, Abingdon OX14 3FE

You will receive an invoice with the first issue of notes.

All our Bible reading notes can be ordered online by visiting
brfonline.org.uk/collections/subscriptions

Day by Day with God is also available as
an app for Android, iPhone and iPad
brfonline.org.uk/collections/apps

All subscription enquiries should be directed to:
BRF Ministries, 15 The Chambers, Vineyard, Abingdon OX14 3FE
+44 (0)1865 319700 | **enquiries@brf.org.uk**

DBDWG0124

All our Bible reading notes can be ordered online by visiting
brfonline.org.uk/collections/subscriptions

The group subscription rate for *Day by Day with God* will be £14.85 per person until April 2024.

☐ I would like to take out a group subscription for _____ (quantity) copies.

☐ Please start my order with the May 2024 / September 2024 / January 2025* issue. I would like to pay annually/receive an invoice* with each edition of the notes. (*delete as appropriate)

Please do not send any money with your order. Send your order to BRF Ministries and we will send you an invoice.

Name and address of the person organising the group subscription:

Title _____ First name/initials _____ Surname _____

Address_____

_____ Postcode _____

Telephone _____ Email _____

Church_____

Name and address of the person paying the invoice if the invoice needs to be sent directly to them:

Title _____ First name/initials _____ Surname _____

Address_____

_____ Postcode _____

Telephone _____ Email _____

We will use your personal data to process this order. From time to time we may send you information about the work of BRF Ministries. Please contact us if you wish to discuss your mailing preferences **brf.org.uk/privacy**

Please return this form to:
BRF Ministries, 15 The Chambers, Vineyard, Abingdon OX14 3FE
| **enquiries@brf.org.uk**

For terms and cancellation information, please visit **brfonline.org.uk/terms**.

Bible Reading Fellowship is a charity (233280) and company limited by guarantee (301324), registered in England and Wales

DAY BY DAY WITH GOD INDIVIDUAL/GIFT SUBSCRIPTION FORM

To order online, please visit **brfonline.org.uk/collections/subscriptions**

☐ I would like to give a gift subscription (please provide both names and addresses)
☐ I would like to take out a subscription myself (complete your name and address details only once)

Title _____ First name/initials _____ Surname _____

Address _____

_____ Postcode _____

Telephone _____ Email _____

Gift subscription name _____

Gift subscription address _____

_____ Postcode _____

Gift subscription (20 words max. or include your own gift card):

_____

_____

Please send *Day by Day with God* beginning with the May 2024 / September 2024 / January 2025 issue (*delete as appropriate*):

(*please tick box*)	UK	Europe	Rest of world
1-year subscription	☐ £19.05	☐ £26.55	☐ £30.45
2-year subscription	☐ £36.30	N/A	N/A

Optional donation to support the work of BRF Ministries £ _____

Total enclosed £ _____ (cheques should be made payable to 'BRF')

Please charge my MasterCard / Visa with £ _____

Card no. ☐☐☐☐ ☐☐☐☐ ☐☐☐☐ ☐☐☐☐

Expires end ☐M☐M ☐Y☐Y   Security code ☐☐☐   Last 3 digits on the reverse of the card

We will use your personal data to process this order. From time to time we may send you information about the work of BRF Ministries. Please contact us if you wish to discuss your mailing preferences **brf.org.uk/privacy**

Please return this form to:
BRF Ministires, 15 The Chambers, Vineyard, Abingdon OX14 3FE
| enquiries@brf.org.uk

For terms and cancellation information, please visit **brfonline.org.uk/terms**.

DBDWG0124